Recent Themes in World History and the
History of the West

Historians in Conversation:
Recent Themes in Understanding the Past
Series editor, Louis A. Ferleger

Recent Themes in

WORLD HISTORY AND THE HISTORY OF THE WEST

Historians in Conversation

Edited by Donald A. Yerxa

THE UNIVERSITY OF SOUTH CAROLINA PRESS

© 2009 University of South Carolina

Published by the University of South Carolina Press
Columbia, South Carolina 29208

www.sc.edu/uscpress

Manufactured in the United States of America

18 17 16 15 14 13 12 11 10 09   10 9 8 7 6 5 4 3 2 1

Library of Congress Cataloging-in-Publication Data

Recent themes in world history and the history of the West : historians in conversation /
   edited by Donald A. Yerxa.
       p. cm. — (Historians in conversation)
   Includes bibliographical references and index.
   ISBN 978-1-57003-831-0 (pbk. : alk. paper)
   1. World history—Historiography. 2. Civilization, Western—Historiography.
   3. Historiography. 4. Historians—Interviews. 5. History—Philosophy. 6. History—
   Methodology. I. Yerxa, Donald A., 1950–
   D13.R354 2009
   907.2—dc22

                                                                                          2008052255

This book was printed on Glatfelter Natures, a recycled paper with 30 percent postconsumer
waste content.

Contents

Series Editor's Preface

The Historical Society was founded in 1997 to create more venues for common conversations about the past. Consequently in the autumn of 2001 the Historical Society launched a new type of publication. The society's president, George Huppert, and I believed that there was an important niche for a publication that would make the work of the most prominent historians more accessible to nonspecialists and general readers. We recruited two historians who shared this vision, Joseph S. Lucas and Donald A. Yerxa, and asked them to transform *Historically Speaking* into journal of historical ideas. Up to that point *Historically Speaking* had served as an in-house publication reporting on the society's activities and its members' professional accomplishments. Yerxa and Lucas quickly changed the layout and content of *Historically Speaking,* and within a short period of time many of the most prominent historians in the world began appearing in its pages—people like Danielle Allen, Niall Ferguson, Daniel Walker Howe, Mary Lefkowitz, Pauline Maier, William McNeill, Geoffrey Parker, and Sanjay Subrahmanyam. *Historically Speaking*'s essays, forums, and interviews have drawn widespread attention. The *Chronicle of Higher Education*'s Magazine and Journal Reader section, for example, repeatedly highlights pieces appearing in *Historically Speaking.* And leading historians are loyal readers, praising *Historically Speaking* as a "must-read" journal, a "*New York Review of Books* for history," and "the most intellectually exciting publication in history that is currently available."

The Historical Society is pleased to partner with the University of South Carolina Press to publish a multivolume series *Historians in Conversation: Recent Themes in Understanding the Past.* Each thematic volume pulls key essays, forums, and interviews from *Historically Speaking* and makes them accessible for classroom use and for the general reader. The original selections from *Historically Speaking* are supplemented with an introductory essay by Yerxa along with suggestions for further reading.

We welcome your interest in the Historical Society. You may find us on the Internet at https://www.bu.edu/historic/ . You may also contact us at the Historical Society, 656 Beacon St., Mezzanine, Boston, Mass., 02215-2010, telephone 617-358-0260.

LOUIS A. FERLEGER

Acknowledgments

As an editor of *Historically Speaking* since 2001, I have been privileged to work with an amazingly talented and accomplished group of colleagues. Joe Lucas, my coeditor, and Randall Stephens, our associate editor, are gifted historians and first-rate editors. Lou Ferleger, the Historical Society's executive director for the past ten years, has worked tirelessly on behalf of the society and *Historically Speaking.*

I am indebted to the scores of historians who have contributed to the publication and especially those whose work appears in this volume. In particular, I want to thank two towering figures in the fields of world and global history: William H. McNeill and Bruce Mazlish. Both have supported *Historically Speaking* liberally from its inception, writing perceptive essays and serving as contributing editors. It has been my honor to work with them. Over the years, I have come to cherish Bruce Mazlish's insight, advice, and friendship. Early on, he freely gave a novice editor two most valuable gifts, his time and hospitality. His support and encouragement have been constant, and his sage comments on the editorial direction of *Historically Speaking* are deeply appreciated.

My wife Lois enriches my life in countless ways. I am enormously grateful for her patience, support, and love.

Introduction

History on a Large Scale

Donald A. Yerxa

M y father's copy of H. G. Wells's *Outline of History* captivated me as a
young boy. There it all was: the history of everything, or so it seemed.
I recall thinking that if I could just learn everything in Wells's volume, I
would have mastered history! Universal history, the grand project of a single,
overarching story of the past, appealed both to my curiosity and untutored
conviction that the past had to be *a* story full of meaning—no thought of
multiple plots at that age. As I became better acquainted with the methods
and practices of academic historians, I was made to understand that my fas-
cination with universal history was naive. No reputable historian should pre-
sume to write such speculative stuff. Still even after graduate school I would
sometimes pause to peruse the impressive multivolume works by Arnold J.
Toynbee and the Durants and privately marvel at the boldness of their vision
and wonder whether universal history really is such an intellectually bankrupt
enterprise.

In recent years some of the impulses behind universal history seem to be
undergoing rehabilitation. There can be little doubt that a striking feature of
recent historiography is the explosion of books examining the past in very
large chunks. Titles like *After Tamerlane: The Global History of Empire, The
Eastern Origins of Western Civilisation,* and *The Europeanization of the World*
appear with increasing frequency.[1] I will use the inelegant term *macrohistory*
to describe this growing body of literature, which includes some types of
world history, global history, world-systems analysis, macrosociology, comparative civilizational analysis, geopolitics, "Big History," and large-scale
world-historical investigations from a variety of perspectives.

Contemporary macrohistory has its roots in the notion of universal history. Although universal history can be traced back to the ancient Greeks,

especially Polybius, and to the great medieval Islamic historian Ibn Khaldun,[2] scholars generally link it to Christian providentialism, which understood God's will as unifying all of human history. As early as the sixteenth century secularized universal histories replaced God with geographic, climatic, and cultural factors, though the providentialist approach never disappeared completely. During the Enlightenment, the ideas of progress and the "cultural development of humanity" eclipsed providence as the unifying theme of history. But providence made a temporary comeback in the nineteenth century, particularly with the work of Leopold Von Ranke, who attempted to combine careful scholarship on national topics with an overarching notion of the history of humankind, which for him was, in effect, the story of God's plan. Other prominent historians—including Lord Acton and J. B. Bury—joined Ranke in viewing universal history as the ideal of historical inquiry.[3]

During the nineteenth century historicism with its emphasis on the study of particular historical contexts began to undermine the notion of universal history. The trend continued into the twentieth century as history became professionalized and increasingly conceptualized in terms of the past activities and interactions of nations. And as monographic studies came to dominate academic historical writing, the notion of a single, overarching story of the past increasingly seemed beyond the grasp of both the historian's method and task. Universal history was further undermined in the concluding decades of the twentieth century with the postmodernist assault on "grand narratives" and, to a lesser extent, by postcolonialist challenges to the supremacy of Western historical methods.[4]

Remarkably while universal history fell out of favor among the ranks of academic historians, traces of the notion persisted—even thrived—both inside and beyond the academy in the various guises of macrohistory. This took many forms: for example, the "pedagogical construct" in American undergraduate education of a Grand Narrative of Western Civilization stretching back to Ancient Greece, speculative philosophies of history made popular by Oswald Spengler and Arnold J. Toynbee, some aspects of the French Annales school (particularly the work of Fernand Braudel), modernization theory (W. W. Rostow and Cyril E. Black), and certain genres of world history that emerged after World War II.[5] A full explanation for the resilience of universal history is beyond the scope of this introductory essay, but the lure of constructing some sort of coherence and meaning out of the chaos of the past surely is at work here. Human societies need common stories of the past to define collective identity and to assist in steering societal activity.[6]

Large-scale historical analysis was given an enormous boost with the publication in 1963 of William H. McNeill's magisterial *The Rise of the West*.[7]

Because McNeill drew inspiration from Toynbee, it is not surprising that his *Rise of the West* was written in the grand synthesis–universal history tradition. McNeill emphasized the importance of cross-cultural interaction (often a euphemism for conquest and the exchange of microbes) and presented a model that located cultural innovation in core regions with diffusion from these to peripheries. McNeill's approach has influenced the field ever since.[8] It gave impetus not only to the comparative study of civilizations but also to various thematic treatments of world history that have typified the field since then: for example, the interaction between disease and civilization; ecological history; and histories of discovery, migration, and diasporas.[9] McNeill's work also has made large-scale world history more attractive—if not always professionally respectable—for academic historians.[10]

Today world history is a maturing field with much of the necessary infrastructure (a professional organization, journal, chaired professorships).[11] As their field has evolved, however, world historians have attempted to distance themselves from universal history's vision of summing up all of history. According to Patrick Manning, "The days of world history as a single, all-encompassing field of global synthesis world history are gone."[12] Since he understands world history to be "the story of connections within the global human community," it follows that the work of world historians is "to portray the crossing of boundaries and the linking of systems in the human past."[13] The influence of McNeill is obvious. But world historians have not been entirely successful in shedding the macrohistorical impulse. In a recent essay Bruce Mazlish noted that world history "tends to be comparative, is concerned with long-term and large-scale happenings, and has a penchant for thinking in terms of civilizations."[14] It is undoubtedly more accurate to use the term *world histories,* as Marnie Hughes-Warrington does, to cover the variety of genres and approaches. And it is certainly necessary to acknowledge the various streams of contemporary macrohistorical literature.

While world history was maturing, another branch of macrohistory emerged in the 1970s, world-systems analysis. The key figure in the world-systems school was historical sociologist Immanuel Wallerstein, who combined elements of neo-Marxian dependency theory with an Annales-Braudelian approach.[15] For Wallerstein the world-system was the key unit of analysis. It consisted of "the whole of a region linked by a single economic network, and divided into the sub-regions of the core, the semi-periphery and the periphery."[16] His work focused on the capitalist world-system that began in sixteenth-century Europe. Other scholars have extended the world-system model back in time to include zones of trade that originated prior to and independent from the European system. Janet Abu-Lughod has done this for the medieval era, and the team of Christopher Chase-Dunn and Thomas Hall has argued for the existence of regional world systems as far back into ancient and prehistory as the archeological record will permit.[17]

Geopolitics—not unlike the metahistory of Spengler and Toynbee—fell out of favor at midcentury. Critics argued that the earlier work of geopolitical thinkers such as Halford Mackinder and Karl Haushofer encouraged military aggrandizement and provided the Nazis with a quasi-academic rationale for conquest. Following the publication of McNeill's *Pursuit of Power* in 1982, however, geopolitical analysis applied to the past became respectable again.[18] A new generation of geopolitically oriented historians especially looked at such things as the relationship of geography to military and political power and the liabilities of geopolitical overextension.[19] Military, naval, and strategic historians, no longer content with "drum and trumpet" accounts of battles and generalship, added their insights to macrohistorical inquiry, in general, and the understanding of the evolution of the modern state, in particular. McNeill's *Pursuit of Power* illustrates how paying attention to the military experience enriches macrohistorical understanding. Recent debates over the "Western Way of War" thesis[20] and the military revolution of the early modern Europe[21] are examples of military macrohistory at its best.

Another branch of macrohistorical literature has focused on the evolutionary, environmental, ecological, and biological processes that have affected past human activity on a grand scale. Although geography and climate were significant and frequently controversial features of the geopolitical school,[22] the historical and ecological analyses of William McNeill and Alfred Crosby were enormously significant in understanding the basis for Western hegemony in the modern era.[23] Relying heavily on the increasingly sophisticated evidence gleaned from several of the sciences, Jared Diamond, Brian Fagan, Felipe Fernández-Armesto, and J. R. McNeill have developed the ecological-climatological approach further in recent years.[24] Brian Fagan, for instance, stops short of claiming that climate drove history; rather, he argues, climate change has been "a major historical player," though certainly not a benign one. For example, Fagan explains how the sudden shift of the Gulf Stream forced people in the ancient Near East to switch from hunting and gathering to early forms of agriculture, how the implosion of the Laurentide ice sheet in Canada ca. 6200 B.C.E. triggered a rapid rise in the world's oceans that separated England from the continent, and how another rise in the waters of the Mediterranean around 5600 B.C.E. led to a catastrophic flood that transformed the Euxine Lake into the Black Sea in only two years. Drawing from an impressive array of studies—from standard archaeological finds and tree-ring analyses to deep ice-core samples, the study of pollen grains (paly-nology), and amazing forensic techniques that one might expect to see on an episode of *CSI*—Fagan's scientific tool kit especially serves him well when he recounts the interplay between climate and prehistoric peoples and early civi-lizations.[25]

Fagan's bold attempt to use climate to understand history seems down-right timid compared to the project of Big History. In *Maps of Time* David Christian attempts nothing less than a grand, unified story of natural and human history.[26] This is a work of breathtaking synthesis. It's all here: big-bang cosmology, the formation and drift of galaxies, the origins of the Earth, the origins and evolution of life and the biosphere, human evolution, prehis-tory, the emergence of agriculture, settled communities, agrarian civilizations, global networks of exchange, the birth of the modern world, and the "great acceleration" of the twentieth century. None other than William McNeill has hailed Christian's Big History as an "intellectual masterpiece," likening it to the breakthroughs of Isaac Newton and Charles Darwin.[27] One cannot imag-ine greater praise coming from such a respected voice within today's academy.

Another subfield to emerge in recent years is "the new global history"—not to be confused with world history. This species of macrohistory pays attention to those aspects of world history concerned with the processes of globalization. Some practitioners go back millennia, but others, most notably Mazlish, focus on the more recent past.[28]

And often overlooked or viewed as tangential in discussions of world his-tory is the enormous influence of religion, in particular the great missionary faiths of Christianity and Islam. The expansion of Islam was essentially pro-gressive moving out from a geographic center, whereas Christianity has exhib-ited a more complex historical trajectory, lacking in the strict sense a single geographic center. Moreover, it tends to whither or grow at or beyond its periphery.[29]

What is fueling all this intellectual activity? Two factors seem obvious: the accumulating scholarship of generations of historians has provided a wealth of information that cries out for synthesis,[30] and globalization and inter-dependency now have placed a new burden on the past, prompting histori-ans and fellow travelers to investigate large-scale historical patterns. We ask a different set of questions than fifty to sixty years ago, and some of these ques-tions force examination of the past in very large chunks. Macrohistory, sim-ply put, is the scale of history most relevant when we think about how the issues now facing humanity as a whole came into being. Interest in the pro-cesses of globalization coupled with an increasingly sophisticated set of tools borrowed from the sciences has made macrohistory much more respectable in today's academy than universal history ever was in the twentieth century.

Despite its impressive productivity and range macrohistory faces formidable criticism and challenges. To the extent it is linked to the rehabilitation of grand historical narratives, it remains vulnerable to the charge that it amounts to a scandalous reversion to history without the details. Many, including prominent practitioners of world history, argue that it is ludicrous to attempt to reduce human history to a single story (or a relatively few). Moreover, some question whether there is a sufficient level of empirical detail necessary to both convey and sustain it.

There are also serious intramural concerns: What are the most appropriate units of investigation? How do we go about periodization? What is the proper role of agency? and so forth. There have been heated debates among those who adopt the diffusionist model of innovation (be it Eurocentric or Sinocentric) and those who champion "the decolonizer or anti-diffusionist model." And in the late 1990s diffusionists fought what could legitimately be called a "macrohistory civil war." Neo-Weberian economic historian David Landes and world-systems macrosociologist Andre Gunder Frank sparred over when and how the West emerged as the dominant economic and military force on the planet.[31] Others, notably R. Bin Wong and Kenneth Pomeranz, while clearly opposed to Eurocentrism, have attempted to get past these West-versus-China / Eurocentric-versus–anti-Eurocentric polemics.[32] Still doubts remain that such a very large narrative can be told without a center.[33]

There are other descriptive comments about macrohistory that could be made, but it might be more productive and certainly more provocative at this point to call attention to three broad methodological—bordering on philosophical—matters that macrohistory brings to my mind as a generalist historian and editor.

The question of scale. It is fair to say that most historians consider small-scale histories more methodologically rigorous and closer to the past "as it was" (whatever we mean by that) than intermediate studies (for example, a survey of the United States in the Gilded and Progressive eras). But can we really posit such a neat hierarchical schema for historical inquiry? If so macrohistory becomes essentially a synthetic exercise, blurring out more and more detail as we zoom up and out from the more microscopic investigations of the past. This, however, is only a caricature of macrohistory. No unit of the past is more essential than another. Just as we ask many questions of the natural world that range from the subatomic to the cosmic, we also ask many questions of the past. And some of those questions require us to study the past at macro scales.[34]

To help us better understand the question of scale in history, David Christian has appropriated the concept of *emergent properties* from complexity theory and the natural sciences. Emergent properties are features or rules that emerge at one level of complexity but are not present at other, less-complex levels. For example, one could say that all humans—indeed, all living organisms—are molecular beings. But we must go far beyond chemistry to investigate the complexity of human cognition or social interaction. What all this suggests is that macrohistory can never be simply derivative of smaller-scale histories. Furthermore, an emergentist approach to historical inquiry would imply that methods and explanations appropriate at the smaller scales may well be reductionistic and unsatisfactory when history is attempted at larger scales.[35]

A fundamental question of method. Macrohistorians today go about their scholarly work using the historical methods developed largely in the West since the sixteenth and seventeenth centuries and refined by professional practice in the last century or so. One does not need to be a devotee of Edward Said and postcolonial thinking to wonder whether this involves a measure of intellectual imperialism.[36] Western-trained historians are trained absorb oral tradition, folktales, myths, and the like with the tools of anthropology, but in the process they inevitably tame the non-Western past by forcing it into Western intellectual categories. I do not want to be misunderstood on this delicate point. I happen to believe that the emergence of historical consciousness, along with science, ranks among the great accomplishments of the Western intellectual tradition, indeed, of humanity. But to the extent world historians are endeavoring to provide a structure for understanding all human history (which admittedly some world historians do not see as their appointed task), it seems ironic to operate functionally as if the historical methods and practices developed and used by the academy in the West exhaust what we can say meaningfully about the past.

To get at this another way one might well ask: Have we arrived methodologically? Historians who ordinarily bristle at the notion of teleology and sometimes even directionality are by and large methodological Whigs—they instinctively consider their methods and practices superior to those of past centuries and harbor no real expectations that historical method will be improved upon in any substantial way in the future. But when we historicize history, we appreciate that of our current approach to the past emerged out of a particular context whereby European thinkers were enormously affected by the huge intellectual stimulation resulting from the overseas interactions of the sixteenth and seventeenth centuries. This was codified in the nineteenth-century academy where the focus was on attaining historical understanding by relying on documentary evidence viewed as dispassionately as possible. If, as some say, the current globalizing moment in human history is every bit as revolutionary as the overseas encounters of the sixteenth and seventeenth centuries, then perhaps an unintended consequence might be the emergence of new methodologically pluralistic ways of approaching the past. Time will tell, but it is an intriguing notion.[37]

The question of utility. What is gained when we attempt to render the past on such expansive canvasses? For some the payoff is didactic. Consider again the work of Brian Fagan. By taking a very long view he is able to argue that civilizations arose during a remarkably "long summer," one of the longest periods of relatively stable climate on record. We have no idea when this summer will end. But we do know that the greater the complexity of human societies, the more vulnerable they become to climatic events. They cannot swing with the climatic punches. While the developed world has gained a measure of security from short-term events, it would be naïve to think that we are now immune from disastrous climatic changes. It is not just drought and famine that should concern us. Fagan reminds us how vulnerable the crowded coastlines of the world, where millions live and work, are to changes in sea level brought about by climatic shifts.

Macrohistory is more than a platform from which to deliver cautionary tales. Tellingly David Christian admits that in *Maps of Time* he is composing what amounts to a modern, scientific creation myth.[38] In doing so Christian intentionally addresses a fundamental need of humans to raise and offer answers to big questions. The academic disciplines have frequently failed in this regard, offering at best fragmented accounts of reality. By carving up the intellectual world into separate disciplines we have made it all but impossible to offer a unified account for why things came to be the way they are. Many historians are uncomfortable with such a grandiose agenda. But the flip side of their methodological modesty and restraint has been a tendency to overspecialize, which in turn has contributed to a lamentable fragmentation. Of course history has its limits, and it would be foolish to ignore them. But perhaps we have been asking too little of the past.[39]

Humans cannot avoid asking big questions. The attraction of seeking patterns and constructing meaning(s) out of the past is an irresistible and, I would argue, totally appropriate task for the macrohistorian. Human societies need common stories, and the grand narrative aspect of macrohistory should be confronted head-on. In 1993 a perceptive historian wrote that world history was "an interrupted dialogue with providence." He was suggesting, of course, that at some level macrohistory is about the meaning we give to the past and ourselves.[40] Seen from this perspective macrohistory is not just historical inquiry done on a large scale but—whether intentional or not—one of the ways that scholars confront, albeit often obliquely, some of ultimate questions of human destiny and meaning.

Macrohistory will never (nor should it!) supplant the monographic and intermediate-level historical analysis that is the staple of academic history. But is it so pretentious for historians to address the really big questions? If humans have a basic need to render the chaos of the past—yes, maybe even *all* of it—into some sort of coherence, who should do the heavy lifting? Philosophers? Science writers? Theologians? Historians? This is not to argue for the enduring value of what Wells, Toynbee, or the Durants—those universal historians of yesteryear—wrote. Far from it! But perhaps Louis O. Mink got it right when he claimed back in 1978 that "the concept of universal *history* has not been abandoned at all, only the concept of universal *historiography*."[41] The big questions never do go away.

This volume makes no claim to being a comprehensive survey of world history and the role of the West in it, nor do its contributors deal directly with such things as emergentism, methodological pluralism, and the meaning(s) of the past. Rather the book's aim is decidedly more modest, viz., to provide a sampling of what historians have been saying in recent years about the history of the world and the West. In the process several of the historiographical currents just discussed are touched upon. The first section includes a variety of essays on aspects of world history. It features an interview with William H. McNeill and his son J. R. McNeill, a superb environmental historian in his own right. The McNeills offer a bold conceptual scheme for understanding world history, and the interview also reveals how William McNeill's thinking has evolved over the past several decades. The second section discusses global history and, like the first, features an interview with Bruce Mazlish, a prominent practitioner. The third section reconsiders Western civilization in the light of world history. And the volume ends with wide-ranging discussion of empire in its historical contexts and contemporary manifestations.

NOTES

1. John Darwin, *After Tamerlane: The Global History of Empire* (London: Lane, 2007), John M. Hobson, *The Eastern Origins of Western Civilisation* (Cambridge, U.K.: Cambridge University Press, 2004), John M. Headley, *The Europeanization of the World: On the Origins of Human Rights and Democracy* (Princeton, N.J.: Princeton University Press, 2007).

2. See Kurt J. Werthmuller, "The Extraordinary Ordinariness of Ibn Khaldun: The Great Medieval Islamic Historian in Context," *Historically Speaking* 8 (January/February 2007): 22–24.

3. Harry Ritter, "Universal History," in *Dictionary of Concepts in History*, ed. Harry Ritter (New York: Greenwood, 1986), 440–43; Allan Megill, "Universal History," in *Encyclopedia of Historians and Historical Writing*, ed. Kelly Boyd (London: Fitzroy Dearborn, 1999), 1244–45.

4. Ritter, "Universal History," 442; Megill, "Universal History," 1245; Allan Megill, "'Grand Narrative' and the Discipline of History," in *A New Philosophy of History*, ed. Frank Ankersmit and Hans Kellner (Chicago: University of Chicago Press, 1995), 153–68.

5. David Gress, *From Plato to NATO: The Idea of the West and Its Opponents* (New York: Free Press, 1998), 9–48.

6. S. N. Eisenstadt, "World Histories and the Construction of Collective Identities," in *World History: Ideologies, Structures, and Identities*, ed. Philip Pomper, Richard H. Elphick, and Richard T. Vann (Malden, Mass.: Blackwell, 1998), 108.

7. William H. McNeill, *The Rise of the West: A History of the Human Condition* (Chicago: University of Chicago Press, 1963).

8. For McNeill's diffusionism, see Jerry H. Bentley, *Shapes of World History in Twentieth-century Scholarship* (Washington, D.C.: American Historical Association, 1996), 15. For a highly polemical treatment of diffusionism in world history, see J. M. Blaut, *The Colonizer's Model of the World: Geographic Diffusionism and Eurocentric History* (New York: Guilford, 1993).

9. Patrick Manning, *Navigating World History: Historians Create a Global Past* (New York: Palgrave Macmillan, 2003), 55–73; Bentley, *Shapes of World History*, 17–21; Michael Geyer and Charles Bright, "World History in a Global Age," *American Historical Review* 100 (October 1995): 1039–41.

10. Bentley, *Shapes of World History*, 15.

11. Patrick Manning notes, however, that world history will remain "an arena of amateur activity" unless it can attract a higher level of financial backing to establish first-rate graduate programs and centers. *Navigating World History*, xii.

12. Manning, *Navigating World History*, 181.

13. Ibid., 3.

14. Bruce Mazlish, "Terms," in *World Histories*, ed. Marnie Hughes-Warrington (Houndsmills, Basingstoke, U.K.: Palgrave Macmillan, 2005), 27.

15. Stephen K. Sanderson and Thomas D. Hall, "World System Approaches to Historical Change," in *Civilizations and World Systems: Studying World Historical Change*, ed. Stephen K. Sanderson (Walnut Creek, Calif.: AltaMira, 1995), 95.

16. Manning, *Navigating World History*, 62.

17. Bentley, *Shapes of World History*, 13; Sanderson and Hall, "World System Approaches to Historical Change," 102–4.

18. William H. McNeill, *The Pursuit of Power: Technology, Armed Force, and Society since A.D. 1000* (Chicago: University of Chicago Press, 1982).

19. The classic work is Paul Kennedy, *The Rise and Fall of the Great Powers: Economic Change and Military Conflict from 1500 to 2000* (New York: Random, 1987).

20. See Victor Davis Hanson, *Carnage and Culture: Landmark Battles in the Rise of Western Power* (New York: Doubleday, 2001), and John A. Lynn, *Battle: A History of Combat and Culture* (Boulder, Colo.: Westview, 2003).

21. See the section on "Military Revolutions, Then and Now," in *Recent Themes in Military History*, ed. Donald A. Yerxa (Columbia: University of South Carolina Press, 2008), 11–48.

22. The climatological determinism of Ellsworth Huntington, which had racist overtones, was particularly problematic.

23. See William H. McNeill, *Plagues and People* (Garden City, N.Y.: Doubleday, 1976), Alfred W. Crosby, *The Columbian Exchange: Biological and Cultural Consequences of 1492* (Westport, Conn.: Greenwood, 1972), and Alfred W. Crosby, *Ecological Imperialism: The Biological Expansion of Europe, 900–1900* (New York: Cambridge University Press, 1986).

24. See, for example, Jared Diamond, *Guns, Germs, and Steel: The Fates of Human Societies* (New York: Norton, 1997), Brian Fagan, *The Long Summer: How Climate Changed Civilization* (New York: Basic Books, 2004), Felipe Fernández-Armesto, *Civilizations: Culture, Ambition, and the Transformation of Nature* (New York: Free Press, 2001), and J. R. McNeill, *Something New under the Sun: An Environmental History of the Twentieth-century World* (New York: Norton, 2000).

25. Fagan, *Long Summer.*

26. David Christian, *Maps of Time: An Introduction to Big History* (Berkeley: University of California Press, 2004).

27. From the dust jacket of *Maps of Time.*

28. Bruce Mazlish, *The New Global History* (New York: Routledge, 2006); Mazlish, "Terms," 37–39. See also A. G. Hopkins, ed., *Globalization in World History* (London: Pimlico, 2002).

29. See Andrew F. Walls, *The Missionary Movement in Christian History: Studies in the Transmission of Faith* (Maryknoll, N.Y.: Orbis, 1996); Lamin O. Sanneh, *Disciples of All Nations: Pillars of World Christianity* (New York: Oxford University Press, 2007).

30. Bentley, *Shapes of World History*, 2.

31. David Landes, *The Wealth and Poverty of Nations: Why Some Are So Rich and Some So Poor* (New York: Norton, 1998); Andre Gunder Frank, *ReORIENT: Global Economy in the Asian Age* (Berkeley: University of California Press, 1998).

32. R. Bin Wong, *China Transformed: Historical Change and the Limits of European Experience* (Ithaca, N.Y.: Cornell University Press, 1997), especially 1–8, 277–94; Kenneth Pomeranz, *The Great Divergence: China, Europe, and the Making of the Modern World Economy* (Princeton, N.J.: Princeton University Press, 2000).

33. Pamela Kyle Crossley, *What Is Global History?* (Cambridge, U.K.: Polity, 2008), 4.

34. In this discussion I draw heavily from Manning, *Navigating World History*, 265–67; the H-World forum on the book in February 2004, particularly the comments of Marne Hughes-Warrington posted on February 17, 2004, and David Christian, "Review of Patrick Manning, *Navigating World History: Historians Create a Global Past*," H-World, H-Net Reviews, February, 2004. URL: http://www.h-net.org/reviews/showrev.php?id=8878 (accessed October 21, 2008). See also Christian, "Scales," in *World Histories*, 64–82.

35. Christian, *Maps of Time,* 505–11.

36. See Ashis Nandy, "History's Forgotten Doubles," in *World History,* 159–78.

37. Although he would not necessary agree with my assessment, Joseph C. Miller's notion of "multicentric world history" is one attempt to address this concern. See his "Beyond Blacks, Bondage, and Blame: Why a Multicentric World History Needs Africa" and "Multicentrism in History: How and Why Perspectives Matter," in *Recent Themes in the History of Africa and the Atlantic World,* ed. Donald A. Yerxa (Columbia: University of South Carolina Press, 2008), 7–18; 58–65.

38. Christian, *Maps of Time,* 1–11. Hughes-Warrington agrees with Christian, but Mazlish believes world histories must function as alternatives to myths. Marnie Hughes-Warrington, "World Histories," in *World Histories,* 8; Mazlish, "Terms," 39.

39. Mazlish made a similar observation in the service of a very different argument in "Big Questions? Big History?" *History and Theory* 38 (May 1999): 232–48.

40. Paul Costello, *World Historians and Their Goals: Twentieth-century Answers to Modernism* (DeKalb: Northern Illinois University Press, 1993), 3–7. Costello noted that macrohistory's appeal to the general public is precisely what is so appalling to many academic historians: "its apocalyptic and moral themes and tone," "its grand generalizations," and "its grand metaphors."

41. Louis O. Mink,"Narrative Form as a Cognitive Instrument," in *Historical Understanding,* ed. Brian Fay, Eugene O. Golob, and Richard T. Vann (Ithaca, N.Y.: Cornell University Press, 1987), 194.

PART 1

World Histories

How to Write the History of the World

Lauren Benton

In one of Jorge Luis Borges's short stories a royal mapmaker is asked to fashion increasingly accurate maps of the kingdom until, finally, he covers the kingdom with a map. This parable is a warning to all historians but especially to world historians, who may struggle more than others with pressures simply to "cover" time and territory. Reaching beyond mere coverage is crucial to the field's development and to its status within the profession. How can we write the history of the world in a way that is not just broad but also broadly influential?

This question poses itself at a time when world history has already arrived as a serious research enterprise. Once the nearly exclusive realm of a few—William McNeill, Philip Curtin, Alfred Crosby, and some others—the field now draws scholars who no longer consider an association with world history as a mark of hubris, a paean to mass marketing, or evidence (God forbid) of a preoccupation with undergraduate teaching. The field has its own journal, the *Journal of World History*, which has seen the quality of its articles rise steadily and now routinely publishes both original research, much of it done by junior scholars, and important synthetic pieces. Meanwhile scholarly interest in the topic of globalization has helped to forge an interdisciplinary audience with an interest in the *longue, longue durée*.

Yet questions remain about the sorts of methodologies that aspiring world historians might embrace and promote. Aiming for comprehensiveness and relying on older narrative techniques are not serious options. Without a conceptual framework the data threaten to overwhelm argument. Otherwise we could sensibly choose to produce a five-thousand-book series, each title evoking John E. Wills's recent book *1688: A World History;* that is, we could write the history of the world one year at a time.

From *Historically Speaking* 5 (March 2004).

Whatever else its virtues world history has not produced a significant volume of methodologically thoughtful discussions or theoretically influential studies. There are, to be sure, discernible methodological patterns and debates in the literature of world history, and some of these do contain lessons for other subfields. Following the title of Donald R. Wright's wellcrafted book from 1997, *The World and a Very Small Place in Africa,* one approach involves alternating attention between global processes and local experiences. This methodology informs a number of prominent world-history initiatives, including efforts to place formerly insular national histories in global perspective. But the approach may ultimately prove less important to world historical writing and to fields seeking a connection to world history than two other common strategies.

One of these approaches we might label circulationist. Its objects of study are the movements around the globe of—in no particular order—commodities, capital, ideas, people, germs, and ways of marking ethnic and religious difference. Like so many tops spinning these circuits together comprise what C. A. Bayly has called "archaic globalization" in the early modern period and what observers of the contemporary scene call simply "globalization" (forgetting, sometimes, that it has a history). By shifting our gaze from one sphere of circulation to another we simulate a perception of the whole of global interconnectedness. Following Arjun Appadurai we can give these circuits names—either his unwieldy labels of ethnoscape, bioscape, financescape, and so on or the more traditional Latinate categories we already associate with established areas of study, such as migration, diffusion, or expansion.

Another approach to globalization in its early and late forms is less familiar but just as important. Rooted in comparisons it purports to uncover the structural similarities of polities that may be distant in place and time. Here the historian finds globalizing influences by surmise and by arithmetic; so many similarities in so many places suggest common connections to forces crossing borders and oceans. When done well this technique reveals hidden continuities. It focuses our eyes not on global circulation but on its imprint, origins, and contexts: for example, status and class distinctions, strategies of resistance, institutions of rule, and nationalism.

Circulationist projects appear to be in much greater supply. In part this is because of a certain transparency of social theoretical constructs related to the movement of people, commodities, and ideas. For example the concept of "networks" has worked its way into mainstream historical studies and has provided a vocabulary for historical writing on topics as diverse as European migration, Third World urbanization, and the transnational diffusion of ideas. In part the proliferation of circulationist studies reflects the institutionalization of regional historical studies and their logical development. For example the acceptance of Atlantic history as a bona fide area of research provides legitimacy—and professional cover—for scholars wishing to map Atlantic circuits and follow them wherever they might lead, even if this means overstepping the boundaries of an already expanded Atlantic world.

Yet it is also true that many circulationist projects remain relatively undeveloped. Thirty years after Pierre Chaunu mapped in Braudelian fashion the movement of shipping from and to Seville, we still do not know enough about regional or global circuits of people and goods (let alone microbes). As Alan Karras's study of New World Scottish "sojourning," Karen Barkey's work on Ottoman *qadis,* Alison Games's research on cosmopolitan English colonists, and other complex migration stories remind us, patterns and understandings of long-distance movements are much more varied than historians of a generation ago believed. Many of these circuits are still in need of documentation, including the movement of both official and nonofficial personnel within and across empires. As for commodities scholarly interest in consumption has played an important role in widening and deepening the analysis of global trade. But here again one has the clear impression that we are at the edge of a vast and varied area of study with much more to explore and explain besides commodification, symbolic capital, and circuits of silver.

As developed and promising as circulationist world history may be, structural approaches to world historical analysis are newer still—and in combination with studies of movement perhaps potentially more revealing. This is somewhat paradoxical because comparative world history has some of its roots in a familiar, old-fashioned comparative approach. As David Armitage has pointed out in surveying trends within Atlantic history, an older comparative history juxtaposed different civilizational areas and sought explanations for their diverging trajectories. This kind of comparison is still with us, as we have been reminded by new attention in the work of Bernard Lewis and others to the old question of where the Islamic world has "gone wrong." We also find it in the continuing debate about the timing of European-versus-Asian economic development that has seized the attention of the so-called California school of economic historians.

There is another strand of comparative history, though, with roots that are better established in historical sociology than in sociological history. This approach analyzes multiple cases involving broadly similar historical processes in order to advance generalizations about "big history." In sociology we think of Charles Tilly, Jeffrey Paige, and Theda Skocpol as prominent comparativists in this vein; in history, exemplary works include Michael Adas's early book on millenarian movements, Philip Curtin's study of trade diasporas in world history, or Patricia Seed's flawed but interesting comparison of European ceremonies of possession. Rather than comparing trajectories and tallying up the factors "needed" for historical change of a certain kind such comparative studies examine the structural logic of conflicts or processes in particular places. Global patterns are seen as emerging out of the repetition and replication of similar social tensions and practices, while these are in turn understood as influenced by familiar global circulationist currents. The methodology has the advantages of privileging the kind of careful case analysis that historians claim as their strength and of placing social conflicts and discourse, broadly defined, at the heart of the problem of defining international order.

I began with this approach in conducting research for my book *Law and Colonial Cultures: Legal Regimes in World History, 1400–1900* (2002). The noticeable dearth of historical studies treating law as a global phenomenon has no doubt had something to do with the imperfect fit between traditional legal history and circulationist models. The book, departing from both, analyzes the ways in which law constituted an element of global ordering before the emergence of international law and the interstate order. In early modern empires, including European overseas empires, and in other sorts of polities, too, legal orders were characterized first and foremost by jurisdictional complexity. Religious minorities, communities of traders, and subject populations were expected to exercise limited legal authority over their own community members. The claims of states did not include a monopoly over law, and membership in a legal community was only sometimes defined territorially. This dynamic of multicentric law was both rooted in particular places and so widespread as to constitute an element of international ordering. To give just one example Portuguese agents arriving in West Africa in the fifteenth century were aided in setting up trading posts by the homology that existed between their understanding of their limited jurisdiction over Christian subjects and Africans' acceptance of the legal authority of diasporic traders over their own community affairs.

Jurisdictional complexity produced both discernible institutional patterns and also sometimes transformative conflicts. Legal pluralism established rules that were there to be broken or changed, and legal actors at all levels of the colonial order proved to be adept at maneuvering through and in the process altering the legal order. One of the interesting conclusions of colonial legal histories is that pressure for the creation of colonial states came sometimes from indigenous actors rather than from the metropole, which in many cases labored to limit its own jurisdictional claims and minimize administrative costs. Over the course of the long nineteenth century institutional configurations shifted—gradually and sometimes only partially—in the direction of state claims to legal supremacy. In this way the emergence of a global interstate order was the product of politics in particular places, rather than the result of metropolitan or Western designs or of some incontrovertible systemic logic.

This example shows that comparative analysis need not propose a model or experience (of capitalist development, state formation, or modernity) to be used as a benchmark for the study of divergent trajectories. It is also important to note that global circuits of labor, capital, and ideas are not irrelevant to patterned social conflicts but also do not necessarily hold the key to their understanding. In some ways this sort of comparative approach builds on the same strengths that make historians so good at placing local histories in global context. Attention to the local *is* indispensable to the ability to generalize about the global. Yet the technique of juxtaposing broad trends with the history of any "very small place" cannot by itself confirm broad insights about global shifts and their origins.

Comparisons of this type, it turns out, may be surprisingly compatible with approaches influenced by postmodern perspectives. Both postcolonial histories and a recent strain of scholarship in British imperial history have analyzed iterative structures within various arenas of discourse on imperialism. Here the echoing effect of structural similarities occurs not across a range of cases but within different facets of a global enterprise. As Nicholas Thomas said nearly a decade ago, a version of world history can be rendered vertically, as the study of "projects" stretching from centers of rule to imperial borderlands.

Both horizontal and vertical variations of comparative world history present theoretical and practical challenges. Comparing structures across many cases may suggest functionalism if one is not careful to emphasize the con-tingency of outcomes in all cases. And asserting the essential similarities of various unconnected arenas of discourse may border on the banal, as when David Cannadine in *Ornamentalism* promotes "hierarchy" as an organizing trope of British imperialism. Although a combination of care and flair may provide an escape from these shortcomings, there is also no question that we are describing merely a comparative *perspective,* not a theoretical answer to the problems of writing global history. At the same time we can affirm that world history may be written with the express purpose of producing theoretical insights and methodological innovations. Coverage is dead; long live theory.

Regarding practical challenges the central problem may become one of sheer effort. Mastering the complexities of conflicts or discourse in a range of places or cultural milieux requires a great deal of time, expertise, and travel to collections, not to mention mastery of multiple languages. Yet these obstacles may appear less formidable as multisited research becomes more accepted by funding agencies and as the boundaries of regional subdisciplines continue to be eroded by the circulationists.

Despite these and other obstacles there are compelling intellectual reasons for making comparative history at least as common as circulationist projects in world history. The approach lends itself to the study of a wide range of social, cultural, and political conflicts and their local-global interconnections. This translates into an opportunity to expand world historical inquiry from its more established base in economic history and its more recent, sometimes disturbingly seductive move toward biological-environmental narratives. Institutions should also be objects of study for world historians—not just transnational institutions, which operated fitfully if at all in most historical periods but global institutional regimes that have emerged out of common cultural practices and patterned political conflicts. And for those who think institutions are a bore no matter how they are discussed, there are plenty of other topics that do not always lend themselves to fruitful study through a circulationist approach. Aesthetic practices and sensibilities, for example, may be widespread without having come to be so through processes of diffusion.

I anticipate—and hope—that the better-established methods of world history-writing will stay with us. We need more well-crafted studies analyzing specific local-global interconnections and also more research into the circulation of people, commodities, ideas, discourse, and, yes, microbes. I also hope that these efforts will be joined by the multiplication of studies that build on the best kinds of comparative analysis, moving beyond questions about different developmental trajectories and probing unlikely elements of global order and disorder.

Unlike Borges's mapmaker we will not have to cover the world with a map in order to understand it. Nor will we be limited to other mapping exercises, such as projecting small-scale studies onto a global plane. Instead of cartography the relevant scientific analogy might turn out to be contemporary astrophysics. Its preoccupation with multiple, unseen dimensions in universes we can only imagine offers the combination of precise analysis and broad conjecture to which world historians might now aspire. And then there's the lure, however remote, of a grand, unified theory—nothing less than a theoretically compelling history of the world.

Webs of Interaction in History

An Interview with William H. McNeill and J. R. McNeill

Conducted by Donald A. Yerxa

In 2003 W. W. Norton published an important book in world historiography: *The Human Web: A Bird's-Eye View of World History* by William H. McNeill and J. R. McNeill. The senior McNeill is a doyen of world history; his son is one of the leading environmental historians of our time. They argue that webs of interaction provide the overarching structure of human history. *Historically Speaking* editor Donald A. Yerxa interviewed them in the spring of 2002 prior to the book's publication.

DONALD A. YERXA: What are you trying to accomplish with *The Human Web?*

J. R. McNEILL: A number of things at the same time, I suppose. On the intellectual level, my dad and I are trying to get across a vision of world history—one that is, we hope, coherent, accessible, and compelling. And our vision, simply stated, is that the means of interaction among communities throughout history have served to provoke the changes that are the main currents of history, and this is quite consistent from the earliest human times to the present. The emphasis is on communications, networks of communications, technologies of communications, and of transport as well.

YERXA: How do your webs of communication and interaction improve upon existing conceptual schemes in world history?

J. R. McNEILL: There isn't a wide variety of existing conceptual schemes within world history, if by *world history* we mean attempts to tell the whole story of the human experience—or perhaps I should put it better—attempts

From *Historically Speaking* 4 (November 2002).

to give structure, pattern, and meaning to the whole history of the human experience. There aren't a lot of various approaches. By far the dominant approach, certainly within the English-language historical tradition, has been to divide the world up—at least over the last five thousand years—among various civilizations. That is, to take elite culture as the primary unit of analysis, because it is elite culture that defines a given civilization, whether that is Egyptian, Chinese, or what have you. And this is the one that informs most of the textbooks, but it is not the only one. In the last fifteen to twenty years a rival vision has popped up—one that my father has done something to advance beginning forty years ago—and that is to see world history as the story of interaction among various cultures and to privilege cross-cultural exchanges, influences, contacts, et cetera. I would say the primary exponent of this view currently is Jerry Bentley, editor of the *Journal of World History* and author of what I believe is the best textbook on the market. But that's about it in terms of coherent visions of world history. So what this web concept tries to do is take the latter of these two positions a little bit further and try to give some structure to the concept of not perhaps cross-cultural interactions but cross-community interactions. That is, people need not be of different cultures when interacting; they can be approximately of the same culture and yet locked in some competitive struggle or, equally, locked in some sort of cooperative arrangement. So we try to give a bit more structure and pattern to the notion of group interaction than does any other vision of world history that I'm aware of.

WILLIAM H. McNEILL: Let me add a bit here. When I was young, there were two visions of world history that were commonplace. One was based on notions of the Judeo-Christian revelation, and it understood meaningful history as the history of God's relationship to men. This was far from dead; there were lots of people in the United States, and in other countries as well, for whom this version of world history was the true one. That is, God's relationship to man was what really mattered. At the core of this vision of world history was the assumption that Christians were the people who had received the true revelation. Muslims had exactly the same view of their world, but it was a different revelation from the same God. And then there was the eighteenth- and nineteenth-century secularization of the Christian *epos*—as I like to call it—that was taught in the universities. This vision of world history was anchored in the notion of progress, interpreted in largely material terms: technological improvements, printing, and all the changes that followed from that, as well as changes of ideas. The notion of European progress had been ascendant up to the First World War. And when I was a young man, the First

World War presented a tremendous challenge to vision of human progress. It contradicted everything in which those who thought Europe was progressive had believed. This was simply unresolved by historians who still thought of progress as the old Enlightenment sort of vision. For them history stopped with 1914 and the controversy over war guilt, and there was no effort to meet this great intellectual challenge to the picture of progress. Progress was one of the great ideas of the Western world, and I was brought up with all that. I distinctly remember the week in which I encountered [Arnold J.] Toynbee as a second-year graduate student at Cornell. I suddenly realized that the history I had been taught had been confined to ancient Greece and Rome and the Western world, and the rest of the world only joined history when the Europeans conquered it.

YERXA: What year was this when you first encountered Toynbee?

WILLIAM McNEILL: It must have been 1940. I didn't know Toynbee's reputation at all. Cornell's library only had the first three volumes of *A Study of History,* and since Cornell did not have any formal graduate courses then, I had free time—something that I've never had since—to explore Toynbee's thought. I was captivated by his picture of a multiplicity of civilizations, each —as he said—philosophically equivalent to another, and this meant that the world was enormously wider than I had previously understood. When I wrote my *Rise of the West* [1963], I was still very much influenced by Toynbee and his vision of the multiplicity of civilizations as the way to handle world history. And then later I was influenced to some extent by world-systems analysis of Immanuel Wallerstein and others, but I also felt that the world-systems approach was also not totally satisfactory. So now here we are advancing an alternative model, the web. The web extends from every word you say, every time, every message. This is the texture of human life within families, within primary communities, within cities, and among all kinds of subgroups with professional linkages. We have, it seems to me, a conceptual scheme that puts the world together in a far more effective fashion than had been true before.

YERXA: Seen through the lens of webs of interaction, history reveals a trajectory toward greater size and complexity. Is this necessarily so? To borrow from the late Stephen Jay Gould, if it were possible to replay the tape of human history from the beginning, would we be likely or unlikely to see the same or similar trajectory?

J. R. McNEILL: Certainly, this is a metaquestion. My answer to it, which I offer without great confidence, is that if we were to replay the tape of human history from precisely the same initial starting conditions—let's say a hundred thousand years ago or a million years ago—that the probability is that we would end up with approximately the same results in very broad patterns. And I stress *approximately*. We would likely see an evolution toward greater complexities of social arrangements and an evolution towards larger and larger units of society. Now that is not to say that we would necessarily arrive at an industrial revolution; we would not necessarily arrive at a world with lots of democracies in it. Those seem to me on this scale to be matters of detail that could easily have turned out differently. But the proposition that the general drift of cultural evolution toward more-complex and larger-scale social units seems to me highly probable. Not absolutely ironclad, guaranteed, but highly probable.

YERXA: What does all this suggest about human agency? If these webs function as the driving force of historical change, how should we view human agency?

J. R. McNEILL: I would say that the webs are the *shaping* force of human history, not so much the *driving* force. The driving force is the ambitions—individual and collective—of people. There's plenty of room for human agency, but as Marx put it, men make their own history but not just as they please. I think this is an apt aphorism. The webs shape what is possible, but the driving force, the initiative, is the opportunities and challenges that people see. Now those challenges and opportunities that they see, what they are aware of—all that is dependent upon the information that comes to them. Information that comes to them comes via these webs of interaction. So human agency, within the context of the webs, works to shape ultimate results. And then on the more detailed level—getting away from the meta-scale and the grand vision—there is plenty of room for contingency and human agency on what for most historians are rather large-scale questions: whether it's the nature and character of the French Revolution or the Taiping Rebellion or of Alexander's Macedonian empire. On these scales, which are pretty big scales for historians to operate on, there is still plenty of room for contingency and human agency. Had Alexander died at age sixteen instead of thirty-three, things would have been quite different.

YERXA: We've seen an explosion of books dealing with macrohistorical themes. What do you make of this?

J. R. McNEILL: I'm delighted to see an explosion of macrohistories. I note that many of them are not written by historians; they are written by journalists or, in the case of Jared Diamond, someone who is part ornithologist and part human physiologist. This seems fine to me; the additional perspectives of people outside of the cadre of professional historians are very welcome. But

I do wish that historians would also more frequently adopt the macroperspective for two reasons. First of all, intellectually, historians, as a group, need to operate on every scale—not that every individual historian needs to do so but as a group. That is, microstudies are necessary and valuable, but to make them maximally interesting and useful they need to be situated and contextualized in larger-scale macrohistorical patterns. At the same time macrohistories are impossible without the large number of microhistories. So both scales and by extension all scales between the smallest and the largest are helpful and useful. But the professional training of historians in this and other countries is very slanted toward producing small-scale studies, and they exist in great profusion. I do not object to that. I do wish that there were more historians eager to operate on the larger scale at the other end of that spectrum.

Second, I think it's important because historians at present have some purchase on the public imagination. This is delightful, but it is not a birth right of historians. There are academic disciplines that no longer have anything to say to the general public, and they exist tenuously, precisely because they don't have anything directly to say to the general public. I'm thinking, for example, of classics, which one hundred years ago was a vital discipline in the universities and is now a marginal one within certainly American universities, and I believe it's true more generally. History, happily, has avoided developing its own impenetrable jargon, although there are historians who have succeeded magnificently in writing impenetrable jargon. Nonetheless on the whole historians still write accessibly, which rather few academic disciplines still do. And a number of historians write things that the general public is happy to read. In order to maintain that situation and, ideally, in order to improve it and expand the general interest in the work of historians, I think historians need to write at the big scale. The general public in most cases will not be interested in microhistories. There's always an exception to that; there's always a market for certain kinds of military or presidential histories in this country. But in general it's the bigger pictures, the bigger sweeps that are going to be the most appealing to the general public. So I am eager to see historians do that and not leave the field of macrohistory to historical sociologists, ornithologists, and journalists.

YERXA: What is your assessment of the present state of world history?

J. R. McNEILL: I'm pretty cheerful about it for a couple of reasons. First of all I believe in world history; I think it is a feasible project both as a teaching enterprise and as a writing enterprise. Obviously I think the latter; otherwise I wouldn't have written this book with my dad. But I believe in it as feasible and practical. I believe it is appropriate as an educational mission for young people in this and in all countries. And I'm happy to say that I think it's getting better in at least two respects: the number of people in the field is growing, and the quality of work in the field is improving. In the English-language community I think that's primarily due to the *Journal of World History,* which has served as a forum for ideas, very effectively in my view. And then as a pedagogical matter the number of world-history courses in this country is growing by leaps and bounds, and in some other countries that's true as well. I don't know if that's true generally around the world, though I wouldn't be surprised if it were. And this seems to me a positive development. Now more than ever—although I think it has always been the case—it would be desirable to educate people in the broadest human context rather than in their own national context or, for example in this country, in the Western Civ context. Those things are actually useful and valuable, but on their own they are quite incomplete. As a pedagogical matter the growth of world history is a very favorable development.

WILLIAM McNEILL: The field is experiencing very rapid evolution. There are a lot of people interested in world history all of a sudden, and fortunately there are some very good minds at work. One of the most impressive, in my opinion, is David Christian. Of course many others are doing serious work. Peter Stearns has joined the chorus, and, if I may say, my son and I are doing serious work. This maturation of world history is not surprising. Obviously the world is a tightly integrated whole today, and anyone who looks at the world knows that the European past—much less the American past—is not the whole past. We are immersed in this worldwide web. And I think it is very important to know how it got that way, which is why my son and I have done what we did. Moreover I think it has the wave of the future on its side.

YERXA: Do you think rank-and-file historians have paid sufficient attention to world history?

WILLIAM McNEILL: Of course not.

YERXA: Why not?

WILLIAM McNEILL: In my opinion one of the problems has been the historical profession's resistance to history that is not based in primary texts. We have an enormous fixation on, what seems to me to be, the naïve idea that truth resides in what somebody wrote sometime in the past. If it's not written down, it isn't true. And that's absurd. But it's the way historians are trained: you have to have a source, and if you don't have something you can cite from an original source in the original language, then you're not a really good historian, you're are not scientific, you're not *true.* The idea that truth resides in what was said is highly problematic. People in the past didn't always know what was most important even when it was going on around them. Similarly we probably don't know what's most important going on around us today. To assume that only our conscious awareness of what we think we are doing is what should constitute history is silly. What happens is a process in which hopes and wishes and consciousness enter, but we don't get what we want; we get something mixed with what other people want, with unsuspected and surprising results for all concerned, over and over again. Now if you take only what has been written down—that which happens to have been preserved, which is a small fraction of what was actually written down—as what historians should deal with, you automatically abbreviate the human career. You leave out prehistory; you leave out all the nonliterate populations; and you concentrate in effect on a very small number of people, often a very skewed example of the upper classes even, the clerics, the literate, which was sometimes very, very small. So clearly I consider the obsession with written sources to be an absurdity if you're trying to understand what happened. It means that people who write books such as ours—which is full of lots of hypotheses based upon little or no material evidence and great leaps of the imagination—may be dismissed has having engaged not in history but historical speculation.

I think this is why many people avoid world history. They have their own Ph.D. to work on, they have to do a book, having done that they're now an expert on whatever it is, they have new problems to look at and new sources to consult, and they're too busy to think of the larger context in which their own particular study takes place. My son's remarks about the importance of world history's context for more-specific history is exactly right. Don't misunderstand me; I don't wish to overthrow textual history, history based on sources. Far from it. It's the interweaving of that with larger concepts that I support. Ever since 1914 there has been no received sense of the whole drift of human history. After the notion of progress was basically discredited, no one dared ask what mattered for the history of humankind as a whole. I think that if we can begin to do that, there will be a great healing for history, and history will be in much more fruitful contact with the other social and biological sciences.

World Environmental History

The First 100,000 Years

J. R. McNeill

"**H**ad we but world enough, and time," wrote Andrew Marvell to begin one of the funniest poems ever penned. Many of us who teach world history feel we already have to cover too much world and too much time. It is no easy business to distill a coherent grand narrative from the infinitude of data. Many prior efforts to do so, both courses and books, make poor examples. One common bad example is to present world history as the story of Western civilization with a few odds and ends tacked on around the edges. Another is to present it as a horse race of civilizations, in which primacy passes from here to there over the centuries and in which Europe overtakes the field in the homestretch. While I think it is possible to present a defensible general narrative of the human career, all such efforts inevitably sacrifice a good deal for the sake of brevity.[1]

One escape from this challenge is to take on only a slice of world history by privileging a chosen theme. This obviously sacrifices comprehensiveness in the quest for coherence. For some teachers this will be the wrong choice, but for others it may be the best one.

Possible themes abound, but in this essay I will explore only one: world history as environmental history. Environmental history as a self-conscious enterprise is now about thirty years old in the United States. It has practitioners all around the world, most of whom write local and regional histories. These may be histories of the processes of environmental change, concerned with fish and forests, for example. Or they may be accounts of what people

From *Historically Speaking* 8 (July/August 2007).

have thought and written about nature, in effect a branch of intellectual and cultural history. Or they may concern the politics and policies surrounding the environment. Rarely does environmental history encompass all three of these forms simultaneously, but it can be done.[2]

Environmental history on the global scale is only half as old. The first efforts in this vein were written in the early 1990s by geographers and in one case by a cashiered mandarin from the Foreign Office.[3] More recent attempts, by historians, have taken on only selected centuries.[4] There is no single place to go to get a handle on world environmental history. So what might a world environmental history course look like?

Let's start at the beginning. For most of the human career we lived in small bands and roamed large territories. It is hard to know much about these millennia, but much of what little we can know has to do with the human involvement with the environment. It was surprisingly eventful. First and foremost at some point our ancestors, whether human or hominid, learned how to harness fire and then to make it. This was one of the great turning points of human history, although we don't know when it happened. Informed guesses suggest maybe half a million years ago, which is before the appearance of *Homo sapiens sapiens*. It allowed our ancestors to shape landscapes, through the burning of vegetation, to suit their purposes: for example, turning forest into grassland better suited to human hunting skills and attractive to the big herbivores that are the most rewarding prey. Fire proved useful in keeping big carnivores at bay, especially at night, improving our ancestors' survival chances. Cooking widened the range of possible foods we can digest, improving nutrition. In short fire changed our ancestors' place in nature and reduced the chance they might go extinct, as most branches of our *genus* did.

About a hundred thousand years ago our ancestors walked out of Africa and began to spread to other continents. In Africa our remote ancestors had coevolved over many millennia with various microbes that fed upon them and with animal prey upon which they fed (and sometimes vice versa). This checked hominid biological success. Once out of Africa, however, our ancestors stole a march on the rest of nature. They left some of their pathogens and parasites behind, bringing ninety thousand years of comparatively good health. They also walked into landscapes brimming with naïve animals that had never been stalked by projectile-throwing upright apes capable of coordinating their hunting efforts through language. They were, in effect, an exotic invasive species in Asia, Europe, Australia (by perhaps sixty thousand years ago), and the Americas (at least fourteen thousand years ago). As invasive species often do, they flourished in these new landscapes, reproducing prolifically and causing havoc for other species.

The species most affected were the big mammals that provided hunters with the most food for their efforts. Soon after people arrived in Australia, many species of large mammals went extinct. The same thing happened in the Americas. It also happened much later when people first got to previously uninhabited islands such as Madagascar (about two thousand years ago) and New Zealand (about a thousand years ago). Sometimes these waves of extinction are put down to other things, such as climate change. Probably the truth of the matter is that both human predation and climate change were often involved, in different proportions in different settings. Climate change had nothing to do with the extinctions on Madagascar or in New Zealand, but in the Americas the arrival of humans coincided with rapid warming at the end of the last Ice Age.

Whatever the constellations of causes may have been, these extinctions had important historical consequences. Australia lost all of its largest marsupials, including one the size of a rhinoceros. North America lost giant sloths, mastodons, camels, and horses. This left human populations in the Americas with very little to work with in terms of potentially domesticated animals, something that would cost them dearly after 1492.

About ten thousand to eleven thousand years ago, perhaps spurred by climate change, people began to produce food by domesticating plants and animals. This transition, long and justly regarded as another of the great turning points in human history, seems to have occurred first in the foothills of the Zagros and Taurus mountains in the Middle East. However had it happened earlier somewhere in the tropical rain forests or along coastlines now submerged (sea level was about one hundred meters lower ten thousand years ago), we would not know. It seems to have happened independently at least five or seven times, perhaps more, all between eleven thousand and four thousand years ago, and to have spread from each point of origin.[5]

Food production allowed much-denser human populations. It required a more sedentary lifestyle. It involved the gradual creation of new, domesticated breeds of plants and animals. Fields and gardens replaced forest and meadow. When people learned to irrigate crops, it came to involve a new connection to fresh water. It amounted to a thorough revolution in the human environment and the human relationship to nature.

Although human populations grew in size, they shrank in stature. Skeletal remains show that on average early farmers were shorter than their hunting and foraging ancestors. They ate less-varied diets and generally ate less animal protein than did nonfarmers. They suffered more often from vitamin-deficiency diseases. Living sedentary lives, they lived among their own wastes and consequently suffered more from gastrointestinal diseases. Their lives, like their bodies, were shorter than those of hunters and foragers. But they reproduced faster than any other human population.[6]

When farmers came to live cheek by jowl with their livestock (mainly in Eurasia), their health got worse still. Some of the diseases that infected livestock evolved into human diseases such as measles, tuberculosis, influenza, and smallpox. Where human populations were dense enough, these diseases could circulate endlessly.[7] Happily to some extent the presence of livestock improved human diet, especially where dairy cattle could be raised (and adult human populations developed the capacity to digest milk).

City life, which began about fifty-five hundred years ago, marked a new stage in world environmental history. Urban populations generally were so unhealthy that they could not reproduce fast enough to offset their mortality and were sustained only by constant influx from the surrounding countrysides. Cities were black holes for population until improvements in sanitation and disease control about one hundred years ago. The natural decrease (surplus of deaths over births) in London in 1750 was so great that it canceled half the natural increase of all of England.[8]

City life also created problems for agriculture. In village settings nutrients from the soil cycled through plants and human bodies and eventually returned to the soil. With the rise of urban populations nutrients moved from the fields into cities, where they accumulated. Carrying human excrement ("night soil") from cities to the fields compensated somewhat for the long-term drawdown of soil nutrients. But the distance over which such measures were practical was much smaller than the distance over which it was practical to send food to cities. So over time cities reduced the fertility of the fields that supplied them, especially cities perched on riverbanks or seacoasts, because their wastes were often dumped into the water and thus their nitrogen and phosphorus forever lost to farmers' fields.[9] Until the age of chemical fertilizers the only way to counteract this nutrient loss was the use of manure from animals that grazed in forests or on meadows. They in effect imported nutrients to farmers' fields. Hence as a Polish nobleman of the sixteenth century so pithily put it, "Manure is worth more than a man with a doctorate."[10]

According to a new and controversial hypothesis, agriculture may also have affected climate. Around eight thousand years ago, it seems, the concentration of carbon dioxide (the chief greenhouse gas) in the Earth's atmosphere began to climb slowly. This came after about two thousand years of declining

CO_2 and when, according to climate models based on earlier alternations of ice ages and interglacials, the CO_2 levels should have continued to fall. How could this happen? William Ruddiman, an environmental scientist and climate historian, thinks it happened because agriculture spread far and wide. Farmers cut and burned enough forest to send about two hundred billion tons of CO_2 into the atmosphere. This may have forestalled the next ice age. Ruddiman also thinks the advent of irrigated rice farming, around five thousand years ago, resulted in extra doses of methane in the atmosphere.

Methane is also a greenhouse gas, and its rising concentrations over the past five millennia have helped warm the earth. These views are new and have provoked mixed reactions. If they are correct, they mean that human behavior has been affecting climate in significant ways for eight thousand years, rather than merely in the last two centuries.[11]

For many millennia agriculture remained the most important way in which humankind affected the environment. Agrarian societies outcompeted all others for the most-fertile and well-watered lands, pushing pastoralists and hunter-foragers to the margins. Slowly, inexorably human numbers grew, and more and more land became field, pasture, and garden. Agro-ecosystems spread. Domesticated animal populations flourished. Forest and other wildlands shrank back.

This slow frontier process is the main theme of world environmental history between the emergence of agriculture and modern times. John Iliffe made it the central theme of African history in his survey *Africans: The History of a Continent,* in which Africans are cast as world history's frontier farmers par excellence, struggling to carve their fields from the forests and keep wild animals at bay. Mark Elvin sees Chinese history in a similar light, as an epic of frontier expansion of the Chinese styles of agriculture, slowly taking over more and more land, assimilating or expelling other peoples, and all the while chiseling the earth into paddies and plots. Elvin assigns the Chinese state a key role in promoting this frontier process, which is quite different from the African story Iliffe tells. But as ecological phenomena the general pattern is quite similar.[12]

Sagas of epic agricultural expansions also characterize the history of the Indian and European subcontinents and the Americas as well. Wherever human populations became large and dense, they did so because of successful agriculture. Large and dense populations (or at least the less well-off people within them) normally felt a need to migrate, to expand, or to set up new colonies. Wherever they had the power to drive off, kill off, or absorb hunter-foragers and pastoralists, they did so. And so, eventually, agriculture covered one-third of the Earth's land surface, arguably the largest environmental impact (such things cannot be reliably quantified) of the human race.

From the earliest times humans also affected environments by moving plants, animals, and microbes around, both intentionally and accidentally, a process we may call ecological exchange. Wheat, for example, somehow got from the site of its original domestication, in southwest Asia, to China by 1500 B.C.E. In times and places where conditions (for example, peace) promoted travel and trade, the spread of crops and presumably weeds and pests, too, accelerated. In the heyday of the Silk Road, for example, China and the Mediterranean world exchanged numerous useful plants and animals: China acquired grapes, peas, alfalfa, sesame, camels, and donkeys in the era of the Han and Roman Empires (ca. 200 B.C.E. to 200 C.E.). Sea routes made ecological exchange feasible over enormous distances. African millets that did well in dry environments were taken to India, expanding the potential of agriculture in the subcontinent; bananas from Southeast Asia came to East Africa, improving the prospects of farming in the moist forest regions around Africa's great lakes. Polynesian seafarers brought a suite of crops and a few animals throughout the South Pacific. All of this furthered the frontier epics of agricultural expansion; it also promoted a slow process of ecological homogenization, whereby humankind altered ecosystems so as to raise a handful of rewarding crops.[13]

A famous pulse of ecological exchange followed upon Columbus's voyage from Spain to the Americas in 1492. After the original human invasion of the Americas toward the end of the last Ice Age, very little interaction took place between the Americas and the rest of the world. The history of the Western and Eastern hemispheres, although showing some parallels, remained separate. But after 1492, as Alfred Crosby memorably showed, the flora and fauna of the two hemispheres mixed together with tumultuous results. Eurasian and African diseases ran rampant among Amerindian populations, reducing them by 50 to 90 percent between 1500 and 1650. Eurasian livestock colonized the grasslands and some of the forests of the Americas. Wheat, barley, oats, African rice, and a few other crops found niches. Going the other way maize and potatoes spread widely in Eurasia and (maize, anyway) in Africa. How different would Irish history be without the potato? Argentina's without wheat and cattle?[14]

The economic globalization that followed in the wake of Columbus and other mariners of the fifteenth and sixteenth centuries brought other effects beyond a flurry of ecological exchange. Commodity markets emerged with long-distance reach. The demand for silver in China drove a worldwide mining boom, most vibrant in Japan, Mexico, and the Andes. Mining everywhere changed the face of the Earth, spurred deforestation, and, in the case of silver, which was most efficiently separated from its ores by the use of mercury, brought lethal pollution. Fur-and-hide markets animated a global hunt for beaver, seals, and deer, altering population dynamics and ecosystem balances in northern North America, for example, where beaver had before 1800 played a key role in shaping the landscape (and especially the waterscape). Markets for sugar inspired the creation of a plantation complex, first around Mediterranean shores, then on Atlantic islands, and on the largest scale in northeastern Brazil and the Caribbean lowlands. Sugar meant deforestation, rapid soil-nutrient depletion, and biodiversity loss.[15]

The process of economic and ecological globalization lurched into a higher gear around 1500 and is still in motion. Overlaid upon it since about 1800 is the emergence of high-energy society, based on fossil fuels.

The Industrial Revolution is often regarded as a turning point in world history as seen from an economic and social point of view. It is even more clearly a turning point from the point of view of environmental history. Prior to the harnessing of fossil fuels people had great difficulty deploying enough energy to get lots of work done. The main way to do it was through human muscle power, supplemented in cases with animal muscle and in a few select locations wind power or waterpower. Most everything, from building pyramids to carrying freight, required muscle power. This was a great constraint on how much work could be done and therefore how much wealth might be created. It also accounted for the widespread practice of slavery in the preindustrial era, as there was no more efficient way to get big things done than to amass human muscle.

Fossil fuels changed all that. They represent a subsidy from the geologic past, bestowed upon the last six or seven human generations (and probably the next several as well). Their ecological effects were and remain enormous. First of all, fossil fuels made the big cities of the industrial era. The fuels allowed enough food to be brought in fast enough to keep millions of people alive. They made the factory labor of the toiling masses so much more productive that factory owners, managers, and eventually laborers could afford to consume cotton, tea, sugar, and other products brought from faraway continents, changing the landscapes of India, Egypt, and the Caribbean. (Initially, in the first two generations, industrial laborers were more malnourished than their country cousins. Like the Neolithic Revolution before it, the Industrial Revolution at first made human beings shorter in stature.) Fossil fuels were a dirty innovation. The first industrial cities, in Britain, were horribly polluted as a result of the burning of coal.[16] Mining coal, like drilling oil, was a messy business itself.

Oil, by the 1950s the main fossil fuel, made energy cheaper than ever before. In combination with new machinery cheap oil made it economically practical to lop the tops off of mountains in search of a few grams of gold. Cheap oil (and chain saws) made possible a sudden spurt of cutting and burning in the world's tropical rain forests after 1960, a major ecological change of our times and one that could not have happened quickly without oil.

The power of cheap energy to enable sweeping ecological changes, to make things happen faster and more broadly than they otherwise could, reached every corner of the globe. Cheap oil made the fertilizers and pesticides of modern agriculture feasible, as well as the agricultural machinery and transport networks that help bring food from fields to tables almost everywhere. Without it the yields of agriculture would be roughly half of what they are, and the quadrupling of human population since 1910 could not have occurred. So it is sensible to regard cheap energy as the defining characteristic of modern environmental history—perhaps of modern history in general —more important even than ever-evolving technologies, science, and forms of human organization. It also makes sense to see the modern period as much more disruptive and unstable than earlier ones in environmental history, at least as far as human-induced changes are concerned. This argument cannot, of course, be extended back so as to include ice ages and major bolide impacts such as that of sixty-five million years ago, conventionally credited with bringing on the most recent mass extinction in Earth's history.

This perspective on world history helps us to understand how peculiar our own times are and in some respects how fragile modern arrangements are. Cheap energy has become a sine qua non for most societies and states. We could not feed ourselves without it, and hundreds of millions of us could not get enough water to drink without it. It is a safe bet that energy history will be at the heart of environmental history and probably world history as well in the century ahead.

NOTES

1. J. R. McNeill and William H. McNeill, *The Human Web: A Bird's-eye View of World History* (New York: Norton, 2003); Michael Cook, *A Brief History of the Human Race* (New York: Norton, 2003).

2. An early example is Donald Worster, *Dust Bowl: The Southern Plains in the 1930s* (New York: Oxford University Press, 1979).

3. Clive Ponting, *A Green History of the World* (London: Penguin, 1991).

4. John F. Richards, *The Unending Frontier: An Environmental History of the Early Modern World* (Berkeley: University of California Press, 2003) deals with the years 1500 to 1800; J. R. McNeill, *Something New under the Sun: An Environmental History of the Twentieth-century World* (New York: Norton, 2000), treats the twentieth century.

5. Peter Bellwood, *The First Farmers: Origins of Agricultural Societies* (Oxford: Blackwell, 2005); Melinda Zeder, Daniel Bradley, Eve Emshwiller, and Bruce Smith, eds., *Documenting Domestication: New Genetic and Archeological Paradigms* (Berkeley: University of California Press, 2006).

6. Mark Nathan Cohen, *Health and the Rise of Civilization* (New Haven, Conn.: Yale University Press, 1989); Jean-Pierre Bocquet-Appel and Stephan Naji, "Testing the Hypothesis of a Worldwide Neolithic Demographic Transition," *Current Anthropology* 47 (2006): 341–65.

7. These matters are reviewed in Jared Diamond, *Guns, Germs, and Steel: The Fates of Human Societies* (New York: Norton, 1997).

8. Alan Macfarlane, *The Savage Wars of Peace: England, Japan, and the Malthusian Trap* (Oxford: Blackwell, 1997), 22.

9. J. R. McNeill and Verena Winiwarter, "Soils, Soil Knowledge, and Environmental History," in *Soils and Societies: Perspectives from Environmental History*, ed. McNeill and Winiwarter (Isle of Harris, U.K.: White Horse, 2005), 1–3.

10. Anzelm Gostomski, *Gospodarstwo* (1588; Wroclaw, Poland: Wydawn, Zakladu Narodowego im. Ossoli skich, 1951).

11. William Ruddiman, *Plows, Plagues, and Petroleum: How Humans Took Control of Climate* (Princeton, N.J.: Princeton University Press, 2005), 65–114.

12. John Iliffe, *Africans: The History of a Continent* (Cambridge, U.K.: Cambridge University Press, 1995); Mark Elvin, *The Retreat of the Elephants: An Environmental History of China* (New Haven, Conn.: Yale University Press, 2004).

13. J. R. McNeill, "Biological Exchange and Biological Invasion in World History," in *Making Sense of Global History*, ed. Sølvi Sogner (Oslo, Norway: Universitetsforlaget, 2001), 106–18.

14. Alfred Crosby, *The Columbian Exchange: The Biological and Cultural Consequences of 1492* (Westport, Conn.: Greenwood, 1972).

15. Richards, *Unending Frontier;* Warren Dean, *With Broadax and Firebrand: The Destruction of the Brazilian Atlantic Forest* (Berkeley: University of California Press, 1995), and Reinaldo Funes Monzote, *De bosque a sabana. Azúcar, deforestación y medio ambiente en Cuba: 1492–1926* (Mexico City, Mexico: Siglo XXI, 2004).

16. Peter Thorsheim, *Inventing Pollution: Coal, Smoke, and Culture in Britain since 1800* (Athens: Ohio University Press, 2006).

On the Global History of Exploration

An Interview with Felipe Fernández-Armesto

Conducted by Donald A. Yerxa

Felipe Fernández-Armesto is one of the most creative and ambitious contemporary historians, so much so that he has been likened to such luminaries as Gibbon, Montesquieu, Arnold J. Toynbee, Fernand Braudel, and A. J. P. Taylor. He is Prince of Asturias Professor of History at Tufts University and also holds an appointment as professor of global environmental history at Queen Mary, University of London. Fernández-Armesto is the author of many books, including *Millennium: A History of the Last Thousand Years* (1995), *Civilizations* (2000), *Food: A History* (2001), and *The Americas: A Hemispheric History* (2003). His *Pathfinders: A Global History of Exploration* was published in 2006. It is a sweeping examination of those who initiated routes of contact that put previously divergent societies of the world back in touch with each other. *Historically Speaking* editor Donald A. Yerxa sat down with Fernández-Armesto on March 2007 to discuss *Pathfinders* and other topics.

YERXA: Would you give a brief summary of your argument in *Pathfinders?*
FELIPE FERNÁNDEZ-ARMESTO: *Pathfinders* is about what I call laying the infrastructure of global history. It focuses on the people who found the routes that connected previously sundered cultures. How have these come to establish so much mutual contact? It has been by human vectors, and it has been done along routes of contact. So the questions I ask are: Who discovered those routes? How did they do it? Mine is a narrative with the implicit argument that cultural exchange has made the world what it is.

From *Historically Speaking* 8 (July/August 2007).

YERXA: Do you believe that cross-cultural encounters provide the spine and organizing principle of world history?

FERNÁNDEZ-ARMESTO: The big problems of our past are: what makes human culture distinctive? Why do we have history at all? Why are our societies so volatile compared to those of other cultural creatures? Obviously cultural exchange is fundamental to trying to answer such questions. But that is not all that global history is about. In addition to how human societies interact with each other there is also the theme of how they interact with the rest of nature.

YERXA: You have written several books on large-scale topics. What is gained and lost when you investigate history on a global scale?

FERNÁNDEZ-ARMESTO: Obviously what is lost at a research level are the thrills you get from writing monographs, staring a living worm in the face in the archive. But the way I try to do global history, you do not lose that entirely. I do not see global history as a different discipline from history, and the world is composed of a mass of details. In my global historical books there are lots of individual lives and experiences, and I try always to maintain close contact with the sources. I do not start with generalizations but with detail, and I build outward from there. What is gained is that you get a far better sense of comparisons and connections. Sometimes when you are working in a very traditional monographic rut, you miss those entirely. There are some great books out there that are deficient because their authors have been unable to locate their subjects in the contexts of the other periods, other cultures, and other disciplines. In everyday life we always learn from analogy, and as scholars we can learn from comparisons. Another thing you gain is the drive to be interdisciplinary. I liken it to ascending to a tremendously exciting imaginary perspective. I believe that the truth is out there and that there is an objective reality to be grasped. I just don't think we can grasp it all at once. It is a slow process, and every time you switch perspective you get another bit of detail. You see the truth from another angle. If you climb to the cosmic crow's nest and try to see the world whole, you see it differently. You see more of it. I think the balance is hugely on the gaining side.

YERXA: The reorienting of maps in *Pathfinders* illustrates your point about perspective.

FERNÁNDEZ-ARMESTO: Thank you for saying that. For example in *Pathfinders* there is a great map of Polynesian exploration. You see it as if you were in a catamaran zooming across the Pacific. How you distinguish good historical writing from bad has something to do with conveying vividly the experience of the past, capturing some sense of what it felt like to be there. And maps can help you do that.

YERXA: You stress the peripheral, marginal nature of Western European exploration up until the sixteenth century and downplay the notion of European technological superiority prior to the Industrial Revolution. How do you account for the fact that Portuguese and Dutch ships entered the ports of the Indian Ocean and the Pacific rather than vessels from China or the Indian Ocean powers entering into Lisbon and Amsterdam?

FERNÁNDEZ-ARMESTO: This is a classic case of the intersection of will (and mind) and matter, of will and geography. The Portuguese and Dutch wanted to go to the Indian Ocean because the Indian Ocean was rich, and they were poor. Conversely why would people already in the Indian Ocean want to go to Portugal or Holland? Western Europe was marginal. There was not any reason for going there. We also should consider conditioning imperatives. The Chinese and Indians were rich, in part, precisely because they operated in the monsoonal environment. That is one of the main reasons they had a longer history of long-range navigation and large-scale commercial and cultural exchange by comparison with Western Europeans. If you are in a monsoonal environment, it takes a lot of rethinking to get out of it, especially because it is guarded from the rest of the world by terribly ferocious belts of storms.

YERXA: You stress the importance of geography and climate, and you seem to downplay culture, as it is sometimes invoked by historians, as a causal explanation. Do you believe that historians have overplayed the "culture card?"

FERNÁNDEZ-ARMESTO: I am reluctant to be lured into vast cosmic generalizations on this: some cultural explanations are wrong; some are right. I am reluctant to accept a cultural explanation for why Western explorers became the world's explorers. I am reluctant to believe that it had anything to do with some inherent feature of Western culture, especially because the ascent of Western explorers was really a sudden event. It happened, historically speaking, in a twinkling of an eye. The rhythms of culture typically change very slowly, and although they might explain all sorts of things in history, they cannot explain sudden lurches, sudden reversals of fortune. For those you have to look at immediate circumstances.

This is a huge problem. Those who deny the autonomy of culture are themselves victims of the culture of our times. It is very difficult to separate what one really thinks from what one is conditioned to think by one's times. In a curious way I think that maybe the single biggest thing that has happened in our discipline in my lifetime has been the shortening of the *longue durée*. I was brought up to believe in gradualism and to think that nothing ever changes rapidly in history. "You have to look back in history to origins" —this was almost the justification for being a historian, that you could not explain things unless you looked back into the deep past. Strangely without much ratiocination we have almost abandoned this notion. We now no longer think that if we want to explain, say, the Roman Empire, we must do what Gibbon did—go back to the Antonines. Rather we look at the immediate circumstances of the barbarian migrations of the fifth century. Or if we want to explain the English Civil War, we no longer go back to the Germanic woods. We deal with the crisis of the 1630s. The First World War is a classic case. Historians used to trace the origins of the war to deficiencies in the diplomatic system of the nineteenth century. But we now tend to think that the diplomatic system of the nineteenth century actually kept the peace, and the cause of the outbreak of the First World War was the collapse of that system. We used to suspect that all of these great events had to have great causes, and the extraordinary thing is that now they seem to have turned out not to have. What gives me pause is: do we think this because that was the way it really was? Or do we think this way because we are in the throws of some vast philosophical revulsion from the whole notion of long-term causation?

I certainly think that the first responsibility of a historian is to look for explanations in the immediate circumstances of the event that is being described. But I am reluctant to recommend this as a unique strategy, because I do not want to fall into a trap of simply reflecting the prejudices of my own age. That would be a failure on the part of historians. One of the things our discipline teaches us is that the way we think about things changes all the time, and the next generation will no doubt go back to some version of long-term causation.

YERXA: Do you in any way subscribe to the notion of geographic determinism?

FERNÁNDEZ-ARMESTO: Absolutely not. The message of my book *Civilizations* is precisely that geographic determinism is an insufficient doctrine. I try to show in that book that you can have huge differences in culture in very similar or even identical environments. So there has to be something else at work. We should not be talking just about "either geography or culture." For me the missing element is what goes on in our heads. Individual ideas can change the world; ideas have power. Ideas motivate us to behave in new ways. We inhabit a world, we imagine it differently, and we work to realize that differently imagined world in practice. If there is one thing that is more important than geography or culture, in a way certainly prior to culture, it is the mental processes that go on in individuals' heads.

YERXA: One of the striking observations you make in *Pathfinders* is that much of the history of exploration was marked by folly. Could you speak to this?

FERNÁNDEZ-ARMESTO: There are different kinds of folly at work. Amerigo Vespucci is a good example. Here was a guy who was a failure at everything. He was an admirable man because of the scale of his ambitions, but he was a feeble navigator, a hopeless cosmographer, and he knew nothing about geography. I do not think he could have found his way around the Boston subway system on his own. In the book I just wrote about Vespucci, *Amerigo: The Man Who Gave His Name to America,* I use the figure of the geographer in Sebastian Brant's *Ship of Fools* as a template for understanding Vespucci. Brant thought that geographers and explorers were engaged in a gigantic folly. He thought that they were foolish, because the world was too big and unknowable. But there were other kinds of folly involved in being an explorer. It is very unusual for humans to want to transcend their environments. Exploration has relied on people who were either slightly loco —people like Columbus and Vespucci, individuals who would never have engaged in exploration if they had known how difficult it was going to be— or social outcasts struggling to escape from the world of restricted social opportunity. In the cases of Columbus and Vespucci these categories overlap. Think of the number of explorers who started out with completely bizarre notions of what they were doing. For example the search for the sources of the Nile, one of the really big episodes in the history of the exploration of Africa in modern times, was a bizarre enterprise inspired by classical texts written by authors who knew nothing about the geography of Africa. And people searched for the Northwest Passage for centuries after it was perfectly obvious that there was no commercially exploitable benefit to this whatsoever. The same was the case with the search for Terra Australis, the unknown southern continent—a perfectly ridiculous thing to do. This is a historical theme you cannot explain rationally. That is why I call it a march of folly.

YERXA: The story of convergence occupies the bulk of your book. Was this process entirely contingent, or were there forces that made convergence a predictable outcome of history?

FERNÁNDEZ-ARMESTO: While it is true that convergence occupies most of the book, it does not occupy most of history. I claim that divergence has been the main theme of human history. Our species has been around for 150,000 years or so. And the extraordinary thing about our species is that we have developed all these different cultures. If you think of it in terms of my favorite point of comparison, other cultural animals, the amazing thing about humans is how different our societies and cultures are from one another. This is the result of 100,000 years of divergence. We've got five thousand to six thousand languages among us. Most species do not even have one. The obvious point of comparison is the chimpanzee, the closest creature to us in evolutionary terms. They are cultural animals, and their cultures do change and vary a little from place to place. But the range is tiny compared to the immense diversity of humankind. So I would say that the main theme of human history is divergence, and convergence so far looks like a blip and is therefore reversible.

If I had to choose between contingency and geographic determinism, I would have to go with contingency. That said there have been a lot of pressures that have driven or inspired history to converge in the last two thousand years, especially the last five hundred years. But divergence has not stopped; in some respects it is continuing. We have seen amazing recoveries of diversity that seemed doomed to extinction. I am thinking of recent events like the breakup of the Soviet Union or the Yugoslav federation. All these historic identities we thought were dead and buried have come back out of the coffin. Look at the resurgence of religious differences. We had thought they would all disappear either in some ecumenical mush or be superseded by secularism. Quite the reverse seems to have happened. Every time you have agglutinative processes—the experience of the EU [European Union] is a good example—it actually stimulates people to rediscover their historic roots and in some cases to invent a new identity that nobody knew before. I am terribly conscious of my Spanish identity, and Spain in a curious way is more plural, more multifarious than ever. This is almost a consequence of convergence, because the threat of immersion in a superculture impels people to retrieve historic identities. So convergence and divergence are curiously interdependent; they play off each other.

YERXA: What about the processes that have accelerated convergence in recent centuries to the point where some talk of the emergence of a single, global culture?

FERNÁNDEZ-ARMESTO: This is a really big question. If there were an end point to convergence and we were to achieve globalization in a strong sense, the result would not be a single, global culture. Another level of cultural diversity, rather, would be layered on top of all the others. It would not smother them; it would sit on top of them like icing on a cake.

But if that did not happen and we really had a single, global culture, it would likely signal the end of history. We would be isolated in the cosmos; we would revert to stagnation, to stasis. I am thinking of the isolation of aboriginal Australia or New Guinea. Agriculture in New Guinea, for example, is as old as it is in the Middle East or anywhere else you care to mention. But change did not continue to unfold, and that has something to do with isolation—Jared Diamond is right about this. If we ever become isolated in the cosmos and have nobody else with whom to interact, we will, indeed, become like the highlanders of New Guinea, from 9,000 B.C.E. to 1925. This obviously raises the question of why convergences accelerate. Once you have societies interacting, they develop new technologies, which allow them to interact with more societies. But it also comes down to ideas; above all what happens when cultures come into contact with each other is that people's thinking is enormously enriched and stimulated.

YERXA: How do you think the impulse to explore will fare in the future?

FERNÁNDEZ-ARMESTO: Although it is true that all human cultures are now in contact with each other, it is surprising how new contacts have happened quite recently. It was only in the 1920s and 1930s that a lot of fairly populous societies in New Guinea came to the attention of the rest of the world. As far as we know now the story is pretty much over, and everyone is in touch with the rest of the world. But there are still cultures with whom we are only barely in touch and those are cultures of other cultural animals. One of the most exciting sciences at the moment is cultural zoology and particularly primatology. I expect we will learn a lot about ourselves from understanding apes and other cultural animals. We are only beginning to study the cultures of dolphins, whales, elephants, and whatnot. The other thing to keep in mind is that although we have completed the exploration of the world in a cultural sense in relation to humans, we have not completed the scientific exploration of the world. My point here is that the environment is always changing, and therefore there are always new discoveries to be made. We have barely explored the depths of the ocean. There are millions more species that we know nothing about than there are that we know about. But even if all of those tasks were complete, the job as a whole would be incomplete because everything would be changing. The opportunity, the challenge of exploring the planet is continually being renewed. I do not want to stop people from exploring space; I just want them to realize that there is still an awful lot to be done down here.

YERXA: How do you assess the projects of world and global history?

FERNÁNDEZ-ARMESTO: It is not in my nature to sound positive or enthusiastic, but I think that world history is the most dynamic subdiscipline in our profession. It is fantastic that so many undergraduates in American colleges take some sort of world- or global-history course. This is a very hopeful sign: in what may be the closing era of American global hegemony, the people of America will be better informed about the world and see the potential of their role much more clearly than they have in the past. Obviously there are things that I feel regretful about. The growing constituency for global history is still terribly ignorant of some of the basic tools, above all foreign languages. There does seem to be a danger in the cohort of us who are teaching the subject that we are getting distracted by debates of how to teach it. An awful lot of energy seems to go into pedagogical research. I have been working with my colleagues at Tufts to devise a global-history graduate program. Unfortunately while there are a lot of undergraduates who want to learn it, very few people are equipped to teach it. But these are relatively small complaints compared with the very great optimism I feel.

YERXA: Is there a unifying theme to your work?

FERNÁNDEZ-ARMESTO: I think there is: I'm trying to understand how and why cultures change. But I would not mind being an intellectual gadfly. I think it is quite noble to be interested in everything and to be interested in successive things. Why not? I do not think I am a particularly interesting historian, but the one thing that is interesting about my work is that I have bucked the trend toward specialization. I have tried to make a virtue of being a generalist. It may be a very small achievement to be accepted as a peer by people who do maritime history, food history, environmental history, imperial history, the history of Spain—but I suppose I can congratulate myself on that.

YERXA: What are you working on now?

FERNÁNDEZ-ARMESTO: At the moment I am tackling the history of language. In particular I have been drawn by what the history of language tells us about cultural formation. It has been difficult for historians to say anything about this, because there are not many languages that are well documented in their formative phases. Typically we do not know an awful lot about languages until they have reached a mature stage of development. There is one big exception: creoles in early modern colonial environments. We know so much about the cultures of slaves in the early modern period. Forty years of really assiduous work has revealed a fascinating panorama of behavior: their work, their marriages, their kinship structures, their religion, their music. We do not know how they talked to each other on the early modern plantations in the New World. They had to craft ways of communicating. Generally speaking historians suppose that slave languages in the New World are not well documented until the nineteenth century. There are a handful of languages that are relatively well documented before the eighteenth century, and some of these documents have come to life relatively recently. So I am looking at those, and I am trying to put something coherent together on the making of slave languages in plantation environments in the New World.

YERXA: What is your sense of the overall health of historical inquiry today? What, other than global history, gives you satisfaction?

FERNÁNDEZ-ARMESTO: I have always thought that the great thing about history is that anybody can do it. You can understand it, appreciate it, enjoy it, and indeed contribute to it without getting a Ph.D.. Some of my favorite historians are lawyers, scientists, and nuns. It is very satisfactory to see historians from my generation reconnecting with the public and not being excoriated by the academic community for actually having something to say to the world. I have always thought that if you have got something worth saying, it should be of interest to more than your fellow readers of the *Journal of the History of Ergonomic Hermeneutics*.

The state of historical education, as well as the state of education in general, worries me. It seems to be getting hijacked by sordid objectives. Funding of education seems to depend on educational institutions yielding short-term payback in terms of the usefulness of what they do. From the historian's point of view this is not a very good thing. The immediate profitability of what we do is not easy to demonstrate. I would like to see people responsible for educational policy returning to the old-fashioned ideals of believing that by knowing more we will be better off, even if the outcome is not easily definable.

Islam

History's First Shot at a Global Culture?

Michael Cook

Collecting coins is a bad habit, but recently I decided to acquire a few Islamic ones. Unfortunately it's a little late in the day to be entering this particular market: too many people in the Persian Gulf (and not on the Persian side of it) have the same idea. But I'm not competing for the rarities. While it's true that I get a mild glow from being the proud owner of an unusual coin, my real satisfaction is the kick I get from putting coins in front of my students. The idea is to take abstract historical points and dramatize them in a concrete way.

Recently I came by two silver coins that lend themselves admirably to this purpose. The most obvious thing about them is how similar they are to each other. Both are covered with Arabic inscriptions and nothing else—and with one exception the inscriptions are identical. The exception is a sentence beginning "In the name of God" that says where and when the coin was minted—though the formula is the same for both coins. As to date the difference is only a few years: one coin dates from the Muslim year 107 (725–26 C.E.), the other from the year 115 (733–34 C.E.). The drama lies in the geography. The first coin was minted in al Andalus, as the Arabs called Spain— most likely in Cordoba, since by the year 107 it was already the provincial capital. The second coin was minted in Balkh, a little to the west of Mazar-i Sharif in what is today northern Afghanistan. In other words two almost identical coins were struck at mints located the best part of five thousand miles apart.

From *Historically Speaking* 5 (March 2004).

By the standards of current globalization, of course, there is nothing remarkable about people doing the same thing five thousand miles from each other. Our present global situation is the product of the European maritime expansion that began in the fifteenth century. Nothing quite like it had ever happened before, unless we care to compare it with the initial settlement of the world's continents by our species. But earlier historical developments had from time to time spread a measure of cultural homogeneity over substantial regions of the Old World. A millennium before Muhammad, Alexander the Great set out on a career of conquest that took him from Macedonia to India. Several centuries after Muhammad, Jenghiz Khan was to initiate the Mongol conquests, which issued in an empire that extended from Eastern Europe to China.

The process initiated by Muhammad was nevertheless more remarkable than either of these. For one thing it started from somewhere very unlikely. It is, of course, a striking feature of the history of the premodern world that the most-advanced societies—the most-complex ones—were not always the most effective in military terms. Again and again the nomadic tribal peoples of the Eurasian steppes showed their capacity to overrun substantial regions of the civilized world to their south. Think of the Huns, the Avars, the Turks, the Mongols, and the Manchus. This may be a paradox, but it is not beyond resolution. These nomads were warlike, and they lived their lives on horseback at a time when the horse was a prime instrument of war. Their nomadism gave them a further military asset, mobility. At the same time their tribal structures meant a fine balance of organization and disorganization. Under normal conditions disorganization prevailed at larger scales, and the tribes dissipated their military energies in making war on each other. But once in a while they got their act together, with dramatic results extending far beyond their pasturelands. There was accordingly a pattern here, unpredictable but easily recognizable.

There were also tribal peoples to the south of the civilized world. Such populations, often nomadic, were to be found scattered across the Saharan and Arabian deserts. Yet here there was no comparable historical pattern and for good reason. In comparison to the northern grasslands the southern deserts were an impoverished environment. They were unsuitable for the horse, and the tribal populations they supported were thinner and less organized. Getting the tribal act together was thus far more difficult in the south, and it is no surprise that it only happened infrequently. The Sahara, for all its vastness, gave rise to just one major episode of tribal conquest. This was the Almoravid expansion of the eleventh century—a significant event in the history of North Africa and Spain but hardly the stuff of world history. The smaller desert of Arabia might seem even less promising, and it, too, only exploded once, in the seventh century—but once was enough.

That brings us to another contrast, the very different outcomes of the ventures initiated by Alexander, Muhammad, and Jenghiz Khan (we can forget the Almoravids). Here, too, Muhammad's enterprise stands apart, this time for the extensive and enduring character of its results. Go back to my pair of coins. One thing they dramatize is the existence of a very large state. Now with the single exception of China, we can think of enormous states as the Poincaré fluctuations of history. The territories of Spain and Afghanistan had never been joined in a single state before the early eighth century, and after the middle of that century it never happened again. Admittedly a single state still dominated most of the Islamic world into the second half of the ninth century, showing a far-greater staying power than the empires established by Alexander and Jenghiz Khan. This difference mattered, but what was crucial in the end was not how long these outsized states endured but what they left behind. The legacy of Alexander's conquests was the spread of elite Hellenism over much of the Near East. This Hellenism was important in its day, and it has left a residue in the Islamic culture that now prevails in the region. But the real future of Hellenism was in Europe, not Asia, in lands that Alexander left untouched. The legacy of the Mongols was yet more limited: the most significant effect of their dominion was to enhance for a while the level of cultural contacts between the settled, civilized regions they conquered.

By contrast the outcome of the conquests initiated by Muhammad was a new civilization, one that continued to thrive and spread long after the imperial state that incubated it had disappeared. By the sixteenth century Spain was lost to the Islamic world, but limited losses in the West had been more than offset by vast gains from conversion. in the East: Islamic culture now held sway from Morocco to Mindanao, from the Atlantic to the Pacific. (I have a sixteenth-century Moroccan coin; I'm not sure they were minting them in Mindanao.) Of course in the wider early modern context this cumulative achievement of many centuries looks distinctly less impressive—it took the Portuguese only a few decades of seamanship to outflank the entire Islamic world. But prior to the onset of the European expansion, Islamic civilization was the nearest thing to a global culture that had yet appeared.

This outcome is surprising in a number of ways. For example Muhammad's message was keyed to a particular ethnic context—the tribes of the Arabian desert. The Koran accordingly stresses that God is sending his message

in Arabic and that the bearer of the message to its recipients—the Arabs—is
one of themselves. It likewise alludes to their Biblical descent from Abraham
through Ishmael and makes it into a charter for an Arab monotheism—above
all by having Abraham and Ishmael build God a house that Islamic tradition
univocally identifies as the Meccan Ka'ba. All of this had meaning for Arabs,
who were being asked to abandon their traditional paganism; the message
was that in doing so they were not betraying their ancestral heritage but
rather reclaiming their original monotheist birthright. But by the same token
this aspect of the message had no obvious significance for the Berbers, the
Persians, or any other of the numerous peoples of the Old World who were
subsequently to become Muslim.

What then made Islam so successful as the religious core of a civilization
that extended all the way across the Old World? Or at least what features of
it look as if they might plausibly be related to this success? Of course it could
in principle be the case that the contents of Islam had no bearing on its
spread, and even if this is not so, causal efficacy is likely to be hard to nail
down. But there are certain features of Islam that are at least obviously relevant. Some tend to the rigid and uncompromising, others to the flexible and
accommodating.

One feature that has a place in the first category is the prominence among
Islamic values of warfare against unbelievers. Whether or not the Koran sanctions aggressive (as opposed to defensive) *jihad* is open to argument; that it is
endorsed by classical Islamic legal doctrine is undeniable. Whether in practice this has made Muslims more aggressive against their non-Muslim neighbors is again a matter of argument, more than likely inconclusive. What we
can say with assurance is that the doctrine of *jihad* has given such aggressive-
ness a meaning that is coherent across climes and centuries. This is not a triv-
ial matter; conquest, though not the ideal way to make friends, provides a
rare opportunity to influence people. If a culture is to bring as much of the
known world as it can under its umbrella, such a doctrine clearly fits.

Another such feature is the commitment to pure monotheism so deeply
rooted in the tradition. Let us go back once again to the inscriptions on my
pair of coins. If we leave aside the brief and businesslike statements about
where and when the coins were minted, the entire coin bite is made over to
God. We read that there is no god but God alone, without companion; that
He is one, has not begotten, has not been begotten, and has no equal and that
Muhammad is the messenger of God, who sent him with guidance and the
religion of truth to uplift it above every religion, whether the unbelievers like
it or not. Not only do these affirmations describe God, they do so in His own

words all of these inscriptions are Koranic. This is God speaking, and he isn't waffling. Of course Islam, like any other literate religion, trails endless scholastic complexities. But here, at its core, we see a powerful and simple message and a notably astringent one. It played its part in the original enterprise of calling the Arabs from paganism to monotheism. It likewise had a vital role to play in the wider world into which Islam subsequently spread. Religious traditions have a way of accumulating large numbers of barnacles as they navigate through space and time; the rigid commitment to pure monotheism provides firm doctrinal ground for movements devoted to scraping off the barnacles and getting the religion back on message.

Against these rather uncompromising features of the religion perhaps its single most flexible characteristic is its lack of large-scale organization. This is by no means unique, but it certainly sets Islam off against Christianity. There are many more Christians in the world today than there are Muslims, and they are much more organized; but by the same token they are also much more fragmented. Centralized power structures can hold people together, but they can also drive them apart. The great ecclesiastical councils of the early centuries of Christianity (and Buddhism) got some people together on the same page but drove others into formal and lasting schism. Likewise popes invite the appearance of antipopes, and churches stimulate the formation of nonconformist sects. There is no reason to expect individual Muslims of a pious disposition to be less quarrelsome and cantankerous than their Christian (or Buddhist) counterparts; the difference is that Islam is free of the large-scale organization that turns such clashes into extensive and irreversible schisms.

How then does Islam work so well without the organization that characterizes Christianity? I don't have a theory to offer here, but I do have a telling example, even if I have to present it in a somewhat simplified form: the Muslim calendar. Calendars are rooted in the natural order of things as we experience it in this corner of the cosmos; that is to say they are grounded in astronomical regularities over which we have no control—such as the time it takes for the Earth to turn on its axis, for the moon to go round the Earth, and for the Earth to orbit the sun. But unfortunately for us there is no neat relationship between the various periods. For example twelve lunar months are not enough to make a year, but thirteen are too many. The result is that cultures have to decide what to do about such things, and they tend to decide differently. Moreover it is not enough for them to decide once and for all; most of them find themselves having to make at least occasional adjustments. This is why the executive decisions of a Roman dictator in the first century

B.C.E. and a Roman pontiff in the sixteenth century C.E. are fundamental to the workings of the calendar we use today. In other words calendars typically need organization to keep them on track—and organization leads to schism. This is how different Christian groups end up celebrating Christmas on different days. It could have been worse. A two-hundred-year cooling-off period and an unusual degree of pragmatism on the part of the politicians eventually enabled the Protestants of eighteenth-century Europe to recognize the Gregorian reform of 1582 as a sensible adjustment rather than a popish plot. The long-term outcome is that most of the world today operates on a single calendar—as it happens a Catholic and not a Protestant one.

Islam, by contrast, has no one to adjust the calendar—and it has a calendar that needs no one to adjust it as long as the heavens continue to behave more or less as they do today. At its core is a thoroughly empirical commitment to keeping months lunar: you start a new month when you see the new moon. As to years you count off twelve lunar months and call it a year; you number these years, starting from the one in which Muhammad left Mecca for Medina and thereby established the Islamic state (hence the year 107, the year 115, and so forth). This calendar, like any other, has its disadvantages. One is that different people may see the new moon on different days, particularly if they live at different longitudes; so some Muslims are likely to start a new month—or celebrate a festival—a day or two before others. But such differences do not carry over because the next sighting of the new moon resets the calendar for everyone. The other disadvantage is that the "year," reduced as it is to a block of twelve lunar months, will not keep pace with the seasons. Because the seasons are of fundamental importance for members of agricultural societies—be they peasants reaping crops, landlords seeking rent, or officials collecting taxes—this inconvenience is a serious one. Normally it is met by operating a secular calendar alongside the Muslim one, the secular calendar often being a holdover from pre-Islamic times. But within these limitations almost the entire Islamic world has been able to operate with the same religious calendar down the centuries and across the continents without anyone intervening to adjust the calendar and without significant calendric schism. At the same time the Muslim era provides a coherent chronological framework for the whole of Islamic history: the year 107 was the same year in Spain as in Afghanistan. No earlier civilization had conducted its affairs in terms of a unitary era in this way.

Of course one might ask how a calendar so elegantly adapted to the needs of a community extending from the Atlantic to the Pacific could have emerged from the local conditions of seventh-century Arabia. If foresight was not in play, was it just a matter of luck? There are long and short answers to this question, but they come down to the same thing: we don't honestly know. In general questions about the relationship between the earliest forms of Islam and its subsequent role in world history can be more than a little baffling. This is not, however, something Islamicists need to feel particularly ashamed of.

The legions of historians who study the rise of the West have not done much better at distinguishing the idiosyncratic features of the culture of early modem Europe from those that were fundamental to its rise to global hegemony.

PART 2

Global History

Global History

Challenges and Constraints

Dominic Sachsenmaier

During the past decade debates on how to internationalize or even globalize historiography have gained momentum in Europe and particularly in the United States. Clearly global, international, and transcultural issues have moved closer to the historical community's center of attention, and the push to do so comes from different directions.

First, there is a reform movement within previously established—yet until recently somewhat marginalized—fields such as world history, international history, and diplomatic history. Partly inspired by research approaches in other social sciences these fields recognize the need to develop new paradigms and methodologies. Second, there are new field designations that seek to develop a more encompassing understanding of the past. One of them is global history.

Global history has quickly risen to prominence in recent years. Some universities have begun to establish positions in global history, a *Journal of Global History* is in the making,[1] and the term now appears increasingly in publication titles. There are reasons for its popularity. The word *global* expresses an interest in the flows, exchanges, and mutual reactions among different world regions. Also in contrast to keywords such as *international* or *transnational, global* does not presuppose the nation-state as a key unit of scholarly inquiry. Indeed in many areas of research such as the study of diaspora communities, religions, and the spread of ideologies (just to name a few) culturally constructed boundaries are far more important than political borders. Even in the case of antiglobal and anti-international movements such as

From *Historically Speaking* 5 (July/August 2004).

fascism, extreme nationalism, and religious fundamentalism scholars are becoming increasingly aware of their underlying transregional or global support structures.

A closer look at recent publications, however, reveals that "global history"
as a field designation does not represent a confined set of research interests,
methodologies, and scholarly allegiances. For example among the newly self-
professed historical studies following a "global historical" approach there is a
certain number that belongs to the tradition of classic civilizational analysis.
Some studies resemble world-system analysis, while others offer macrostruc-
tural comparisons. It remains to be seen whether global history will be established as a more specific, targeted subfield or whether it will remain an
umbrella term for a large and often incompatible number of approaches.

Certainly there are a number of historians seeking to narrow down the
understanding of global history to a limited time frame and set of approaches.
Some historians make an effort to distinguish global history from world history. For example they argue that unlike the historically somewhat problematic term *world, globe* does not smack of Western centrism. They point out
that world history has traditionally focused on the premodern period and
taken civilizations as the main units of analysis. By contrast global history
could designate a research field exploring the world's historically increasing
interconnectedness in terms of cross-regional exchanges and flows. According to this approach global history deals with the history of globalization
processes and their antecedents that can be traced back to the very beginnings
of human migration from Africa to Eurasia and eventually to all the continents. Other scholars understand global history as a field that investigates a
more recent period when world regions became tightly entangled into a
global nexus of exchanges, which is sometimes referred to as a "global epoch"
(a term coined by Bruce Mazlish) in history.

No matter when one sets the beginning of a period studied by global history, it is certainly true that especially the past two hundred years have not
been studied sufficiently from a global perspective. This is somewhat ironic,
given the shrinking of real and imaginary spaces as well as the ever-increasing
levels of cross-cultural connections during the nineteenth and twentieth centuries. Needless to say there are many key topics worth approaching from a
global perspective. These include the global spread of political ideologies,
visions of world order, consumption patterns, artistic trends and fashions,
lifestyles, and city cultures, as well as the worldwide spread of certain social,
generational, and even cultural identities. One of several particularly interesting fields of inquiry is the close interconnection between global flows of ideas

and their respective sociopolitical carriers. More specifically we need to study in greater detail how certain segments of society, such as "the intellectuals" or "the proletariat," constructed themselves according to real or perceived global trends.

If research remains confined to concise topics, steering historiography into the rather unknown ocean surrounding the isles of solidly explored nation-states and regions does not aim at all-encompassing visions reaching across time and space. It is by no means tantamount to arguing for a universalization or even Westernization of the current world. In any case the shift to multipolar and global perspectives necessitates further intensive methodological debates on how to balance the gains of a global perspective with the potential losses in local sensitivity. Any historiographic research with a decidedly global perspective will also have to find ways to balance the universal and the particular. It has to be sensitive to both the inner diversity of global structures and the global dimension of many local forces. In sociology new approaches such as the idea of "multiple modernities" or the assumption of "glocalizing" processes head in a similar direction.

But what historian would actually be able to conduct studies that would be historically detailed, regionally sensitive, and globally aware? Another myriad of edited volumes with single chapters shedding light on different regional experiences will not provide an answer. As has often been pointed out such essay collections tend to reinforce a regional bias instead of integrating different regional experiences into a superordinate, transcultural vision. Merely amassing additional area perspectives will most certainly not internationalize historiography in any prolific way. What makes it hard to open historical research to the study of the world at large is not only the structure of most history departments but also some disciplinary value systems and mentalities.

It is helpful to keep in mind that in the core social sciences (that is, sociology, government, and economics) several disciplinary patterns of *longue durée* facilitated the sudden growth of studies with a global focus. Crucial in this regard was the nomothetic tradition of these fields with their historic role of describing universal patterns in human development. Part of this universalizing outlook was a wide acceptance of macroperspectives. In the past such models tended to be too homogenizing and Eurocentric. For the core social sciences the current methodological challenge is thus not so much to discover global perspectives but rather how to de-Westernize and pluralize their approaches. Of a very different nature are the confinements of historiography. We should consider that history as an academic discipline has had particularly close ties to the nation-state. Few historians are involved in national identity-building, but certain remnants of this tradition survive. Generally speaking historians distrust macrolevel approaches and favor instead detailed work with a narrow scope. For this reason neither the so-called philosophies of history by Arnold J. Toynbee or Oswald Spengler nor modernization theories or world-system analysis generated broad support among historians. Certainly in the United States and other countries but especially in Germany after World War II social historians mobilized against the predominant historicist mentality with its high appreciation of philology and close readings of texts. However even though they adopted a methodology and agenda that was closely related to the quantitative methods of the core social sciences, most social historians confined their work to the same cultural boundaries as their predecessors.

Another remnant of historiography's particularistic heritage is that most historians confine their research and teaching to one or two nation-states. Faced with, on the one hand, the need to widen its scope and, on the other, its commitment to solid source work historiography finds itself in a gridlock. One way to retain the tradition of detailed analysis while exploring global fields of inquiry is to work in teams. However genuine teamwork is still highly unusual in historiography and even in the social sciences in general. If we want to produce at least some accounts that seek to understand worldwide constellations and processes, we should try to experiment with group authorship. It is possible to imagine different area experts jointly developing a shared set of questions and a common methodological framework.

Negotiated methodologies may lead to promising new insights, particularly because different regional studies still apply rather-divergent methodologies to related historical phenomena. For example historians of Europe and East Asia tend to apply different sets of questions to twentieth-century transformations of political cultures in both world regions. However both in Europe and East Asia certain developments such as the advent of mass media, mass mobilization, and political radicalism were indeed related to similar structural transformations and influences. A methodological synthesis can thus produce more than a coherent framework for a global analysis—it can lead to cross-fertilizations between area-specific research approaches.

But there is a price to pay for experiments with genuine group research. For example there is the question of historical narrative and especially the problem of authorship. A derivative issue, which may even be of central concern for younger scholars who have not yet established themselves, is that the academic reward system does not truly acknowledge collective efforts. In that way coauthored publications can only remain a byproduct of some personal research project. But even strictly personal research projects can aim at sketching out global constellations by focusing on two or three regions as probes of a wider constellation. In other words a small number of national or cultural cases could be studied making use of primary-source material and then related to other regional experiences, for which the historian would necessarily have to rely on secondary literature. Such studies could provide an important bridge between the disparate disciplines of historical comparison and the historiography of intercultural relations, transfers, or encounters. They embed the detailed analysis of a limited number of cases into a larger, global perspective.

Certainly the study of global processes blurs previously established academic boundaries, and many projects with a global scope will be interdisciplinary in nature. However different academic fields are likely to retain some aspects of their disciplinary cultures, and historiography can certainly add its own elements to the rapidly expanding study of global flows and structures in the widest sense. Historiography can contribute a narrative tradition, which tends to be filled with less academic jargon than the literature of other fields and is less captive to rigid theoretical frameworks. And it can provide meticulous source work and an appreciation of local details, which are essential for understanding global dynamics and constellations in their full complexity.

NOTE

1. *New Global Studies* was launched in 2007.

From Psychohistory to New Global History

An Interview with Bruce Mazlish

Conducted by Donald A. Yerxa

MIT intellectual historian Bruce Mazlish began his career with a splash. Soon after receiving his Ph.D. from Columbia University he joined Jacob Bronowski to write the widely acclaimed *The Western Intellectual Tradition* (1960). Since then he has been identified with several seemingly disparate intellectual pursuits: psychohistory, the history of the social sciences, and most recently global history. Along the way Mazlish wrote and edited several important books including his edited volume *Psychoanalysis and History* (1971), *James and John Stuart Mill: Father and Son in the Nineteenth Century* (1975), *A New Science: The Breakdown of Connections and the Birth of Sociology* (1989), *The Fourth Discontinuity: The Co-Evolution of Humans and Machines* (1993), and *The Uncertain Sciences* (1998). He helped found the premiere journal of historical philosophy, *History and Theory.* Now his efforts are focused on organizing the field of "new global history." *Historically Speaking* editor Donald A. Yerxa sat down with Mazlish in his Cambridge, Massachusetts, home in March 2004 and asked him to comment on his present involvement with new global history.

DONALD A. YERXA: Your most recent work is in the field of global history. How did that come about?

BRUCE MAZLISH: Like many historians I had become aware of the need to get past our Eurocentric view of history. While I applauded the effort of world history, I never practiced it as such. I had some reservations. Much of

From *Historically Speaking* 5 (July/August 2004).

what I saw under the heading of world history was taking a basic European narrative and adding a chapter on Asia or Africa. I didn't see much concern for the explanatory and theoretical aspects of the enterprise. So I remained an interested bystander. Around 1988 my wife, who is a development economist, was running a faculty seminar on global issues at Boston University. She asked me to attend, and I learned that something called "globalization" was happening. That seemingly sudden awareness came on top of a longstanding interest of mine in modernity, a major way of characterizing our more-recent history. So I became intrigued with looking at globalization from a historical perspective. Rather dauntingly none of my colleagues seemed to be interested in this subject.

I asked myself how one would conceptualize a global history. It seemed to me that the fact that we had stepped into space was hugely significant. Back in the 1960s I had been asked by the American Academy to be part of a project assessing the secondary and tertiary effects of the space program. I was to explore historical analogies to the space program. I ended up suggesting that we consider the analogy of the railroads rather than the more obvious one of the age of exploration. So I edited a book called *The Railroad and the Space Program* (1965) with some wonderful people contributing, people like Alfred Chandler and Leo Marx. I happen to think that it is the best single volume on the nineteenth-century American railroad.

At any rate space had been very much on my mind. And I began to see globalization differently from those studying it from economic or cultural perspectives. It seemed to me that a number of factors had emerged with an intensity and a synchronicity that while deeply rooted in the past were unprecedented. After World War II the communications revolution brought about by satellites made possible an acceleration in the growth of both multinational corporations and nongovernmental organizations. It also made possible a number of other things: the environmental movement, where we see the Earth as a whole not as a collection of nation-states; the human rights movement; world music, et cetera. In fact enough has emerged that I think we need to redefine the social sciences in the light of globalization. We must go beyond the concept of modernity, which was based on the model of the nation-state. Now we must make a major imaginative leap.

It seemed to me that enough was happening to justify the argument that humanity was indeed entering a new global epoch. So I organized a series of conferences on global history in an effort to begin research on specific aspects of globalization. I'll mention only one of these projects. Open an atlas, what do you see? Nation-states and empires. Well, according to the United Nations, of the one hundred largest possessors of GDP in the world, fifty-one are multinational corporations. While one has to be careful how one handles statistics, on that index some multinational corporations are wealthier than most of the world's nation-states. They have enormous power. So I had the idea to "map" multinational corporations to give them visual representation. I secured funding for the project, and the New Global History initiative has recently produced a book called *Global Inc.* It is illuminating. We include, for example, a chart showing the growth of the multinationals from around 1600 (Dutch and English East India companies) to the present, and the curve rises precipitously in the post–World War II era. When we started the project in 1998, there were over fifty-three thousand multinationals, and when we finished the project in 2000, there were over sixty-three thousand multinational corporations. When you dig further, you find all sorts of interesting things, such as that the market share of multinationals held in the United States has diminished by 40 percent in the last twenty-five years. This has implications for all those questions surrounding the nature of globalization: is it really just Americanization, et cetera?

YERXA: How do you distinguish between global history and world history?

MAZLISH: There is a tremendous amount of confusion on this. Though they are often used synonymously, one has to make a distinction between world history and global history. Global history pays attention to that aspect of world history concerned with the processes of globalization. But to indicate the nature of the research project now underway, I began to use the term *new global history,* which focuses on the recent past of the present-day processes of globalization. There are now about twenty people who work closely in the field, and we have, among other things, a Web site, www.newglobal-history.org; an Internet discussion group, and a list of planned conferences along with a number that have already taken place. But in order to establish new global history as a field—the problem of institutionalization—we need to set up an association and create a new journal, and we are working toward this.[1]

YERXA: Does new global history (or NGH) primarily examine current globalizing processes in historical perspective, or does it investigate processes that can only be fully understood globally?

MAZLISH: Your question touches on an important matter. NGH is a new field struggling to define itself. My colleague at Harvard Akira Iriye and I are editing *The Global History Reader,* to be published by Routledge.[2] This comes out of a course we taught jointly at Harvard "The New Global History," which focused on the post–World War II period. Historians get scared that we are doing contemporary history, but Herodotus did contemporary history. We have got to deal with the issues of enormous importance to our existence, and if they happen to involve practicing contemporary history, so be it. With that said the first part of your question would pertain. Thus if one were speaking of migrations, one would have to go back to the diasporas of the past to understand what is involved in many migrations today. Although the focus is very pronouncedly on the last fifty or sixty years, in principle new global history looks at the globalization process over extended periods of time.

YERXA: Whereas traditional history was oriented around the nation-state, and world history has explored a variety of units of investigation—such as empires, civilizations, and processes—what are the units of investigation of NGH? Is it the processes themselves or the agents behind the processes that interest you?

MAZLISH: That is an excellent question. As I have indicated, historians have tended to view the nation-state as the traditional actor in history. There is no reason why that has to be abandoned as long as we see the nation-state in a larger, global perspective. The nation-state is not going to disappear, but many of its tasks are now somewhere else. For example nongovernmental organizations (NGOs) are essential to most nation-states. Or if one were investigating environmental or human rights questions, one would certainly have to look both at NGOs and multinational corporations. So these have become the new actors.

You mentioned empires, and I immediately think of the growing literature surrounding the notion of a new American empire. But that would not be the focus of NGH. As to civilizations I am very dubious about the whole notion. It just so happens, by the way, that I have written a small book *Civilization and Its Contents*.[3] The book opens with a straightforward historical question: when did the reified term *civilization* first emerge? It was in 1756 with the French physiocrat Mirabeau the Elder.

More to your question, civilizations do not throw up satellites.

YERXA: You have been very careful to avoid anything smacking of determinism. So how does NGH account for contingency and human agency?

MAZLISH: Something called globalization may or may not have been occurring in the past. And going back we can draw a line that shows how humans have become more connected and interdependent over time. If we can understand this development, as best we can, then we have a responsibility to exercise human agency. I feel obliged to try to push globalization in a moral direction, and I am fully aware that the present [George W. Bush] administration has a very contrary notion. It talks about a globalized world, but it is mere rhetoric. The emphasis is on American national security and sovereignty. The Bush administration is so far behind in its understanding of history that it makes me want to cry. That doesn't mean we cannot have differences about globalization. There is a very dark side to it. In any event there are enormously powerful forces pushing toward increased globalization. Indigenous people are probably losing out badly, while the women's rights movement is benefiting from globalization.

YERXA: What training and methodological skills are needed to do NGH, and how does one get credentialed in the field?

MAZLISH: As yet there is no graduate program in NGH. I am sure there will be shortly. A number of institutions offer programs in global studies, and Dominic Sachsenmaier [whose essay precedes this interview in the current volume] was appointed to the first academic position specifically described as global history, at the University of California, Santa Barbara. There will be more of those in the future. A sign of the growth in this area can be seen in the course that Iriye and I gave at Harvard. The first year it was supposed to be a "conference course," a small discussion course of six or seven undergraduate students. We had double that number, and four of them were graduate students. We were asked to give it again as a general course, and the enrollment was in the upper thirties, fourteen of whom were graduate students. They were begging for training, but what does it mean to be trained in NGH? The problem is that academics cut up the phenomenon of globalization for their own convenience, but that's not the real world. The economic, cultural, and political are constantly intermixing. So right now the only way to learn global history is by doing global history, by doing it on the job.

YERXA: Is it then necessarily a collaborative field?

MAZLISH: There are those who feel that it is. I agree that the research will have to be collaborative, but ultimately individual minds have to pull this all together.

YERXA: Why is large-scale history so robust these days?

MAZLISH: Part of the answer has to be that as we are experiencing globalization, we are prone to ask new questions of the past, questions that often look at large-scale processes or developments. But the same impulses that push us to the macro also tempt many people to go to the micro. Part of the lure of anthropology is nostalgic. "Why can't those people stay that way?" And that same dynamic is present in some of the interest in microhistory.

YERXA: What do you make of attempts by people like Jared Diamond or the so-called Big Historians to use sweeping scientific explanations to address the big questions of history?

MAZLISH: There is a great temptation on the part of the human sciences to mimic the natural sciences. Lately this has taken the form of relying on sociobiological explanations. This positivist approach is largely misguided, because it doesn't work. No doubt we need the evolutionary framework, but I don't think that using specific evolutionary theories devised for the natural world works when applied to the human history. Incidentally, I think that Diamond's *Guns, Germs, and Steel* is a major achievement, a kind of exception to the rule. But it falters when he reaches modern times.) I do think that the Big History approach of Fred Spier and David Christian is interesting and provocative, but they are flying so high above the ground most of us are trying to till that there is a disconnect.

YERXA: Are the big questions eliminated because we have ruled them out of bounds methodologically? Or do they persist, regardless of historians' skittishness, because humans necessarily use the past to establish meaning?

MAZLISH: I think they do persist because human beings are desperate to make sense out of things. I tend to operate on a more modest and empirical level.

YERXA: What do you see as the relationship between the various levels of historical inquiry?

MAZLISH: I believe that you cannot do good local history anymore without paying attention to the interaction with the global. And vice versa. It's all connected. So if you are studying a small town in upstate New York, and you find that in the past there was an increase in unemployment, you might look to where else in America the jobs went. Nowadays, you have to look at the global context of such things. You cannot separate the local from the national from the global.

YERXA: Are historians asking the right questions?

MAZLISH: The first thing that must be said is that there is some wonderfully creative work going on in history. But we still have a long way to go, and in part this is a function of the way the field has been institutionalized. While our world has changed, historians haven't absorbed that fact. The nation-state has been the main orientation of historians; the training of historians and the resources committed to history still reflect this. So many of the things that concern us today—the environment, currencies, jobs, et cetera—are global, and we don't have the analytic categories to understand these. How do you make the jump, especially when the profession still rewards the monograph based on archival material? To be sure the monograph is the bedrock of historical inquiry, but we need to redefine what we mean by an archive nowadays.

What makes history so fascinating to me is that it is telling us who we are, what we are, what we have been, and where we are going. I may overstate my case here, but I think it is wrong to write a monograph without asking where it all fits into answering the so-called large questions. We all like a good story, but that seems like a secondary assignment for the historian. Having said this I must assert that I do not believe in teleology, that history is heading in a particular direction. On the other hand we do have a responsibility to identify the large currents that are swirling toward a particular outcome, globalization being one of them.

YERXA: On a personal level, what has the study of history meant to you?

MAZLISH: It has given me a sense of meaning of what it is to be a human being. It situates me. I am different from, say, Voltaire in the eighteenth century, and yet as a human being I share many things with him as well. At another level since I don't have a religious view of immortality, I derive meaning from history. I know I am going to die one day, but my life has meaning because it joins with that of all my fellow humans.

NOTES

1. *New Global Studies* was launched in 2007.
2. It was published later in 2004.
3. Bruce Mazlish, *Civilization and Its Contents* (Stanford, Calif.: Stanford University Press, 2004).

Globalization and World History

Robbie Robertson

G lobalization is often regarded as a very modern condition. It is not. Humans have experienced at least three very distinct waves of globalization during the last five centuries. These waves have each transformed the context in which humans live and the ways that humans view themselves and their world. In particular they have made possible the development of global consciousness. It is likely that human futures will be increasingly linked to the evolution of global perspectives and their applications.

Understanding Globalization

Traditionally historians have not engaged in debates on globalization as much as academics in other disciplines. This has been unfortunate. The lack of historical depth in many studies on globalization weakens their claims to validity and limits our understanding of globalization. If we are to strengthen global awareness, we must contextualize globalization historically.

To do this is not an easy matter because we are still captive to ways of thinking that derived from earlier responses to globalization. These earlier responses stressed nationalism and the role of the state in national development. In addition perspectives developed by transnational entities increasingly now monopolize our views on globalization. They stress that globalization is very recent (a result of their activities) and economically driven. Historical perspectives, however, enable more inclusive and richer meanings of globalization.

In *The Three Waves of Globalization* I describe globalization as the outcome of human interconnections. Human-interconnections-as-globalization is a very different beast from its corporate brand. This globalization is about

From *Historically Speaking* 5 (July/August 2004).

human empowerment and democratization, a focus that for the historian can rescue the human story from the parochialisms of the past and provide glimpses of humanity's common history and shared interests. World history can have no greater goal.

Three waves of globalization have enveloped humanity. Each wave produced new forms of interconnections and generated new synergies that in time led to its own transformation. No wave has ever been the product of one civilization or one culture alone, despite our tendency to conflate globalization and Westernization. Waves encompass many cultures; they enable interaction and cross-fertilization. No wave has ever been the creature of one country alone, although at times hegemons and would-be hegemons have tried to monopolize them. Such attempts at exclusivity have always been counterproductive. By reducing interconnections they smothered globalization and generated greater instability. War and conquest became attractive alternatives. The first wave faltered during the late eighteenth century for this reason; the second wave similarly collapsed in the early twentieth century. The same prospect could face our current third wave.

Like earlier waves the third wave is dynamic but it possesses characteristics that also make it qualitatively different. Its main difference can be summed up in one word that suggests the emergence of something greater than the accident of interconnections. That word is *globalism,* meaning a conscious process of globalization or a set of policies designed specifically to effect global rather than international relationships. Thus it has been possible after 1944 to speak of American globalism. No such globalism existed under British hegemony in the nineteenth century. Britain never pursued strategies designed to engender global relations. Its goals were always nationally or imperially focused. The same might be said of the United States, but its globalism set in place institutions capable, in theory if not always in practice, of independently developing global policies. The difference lies in part in the United States' desire not to repeat the mistakes made by major powers during the second wave. But it lay also in the fact that American hegemony coincided with a remarkable process of democratization that radically transformed all societies (although not equally) and enabled the emergence of very different and dynamic structures for global cooperation.

To understand this changing character of globalization we need to acknowledge that interconnectedness and its consequences have never been features of the contemporary era alone. They are in fact integral to an understanding of world history. Indeed the records of the past demonstrate their centrality as motors for human change.

Managing Globalization

Managing change has never come easily to human societies, but increased linkages between communities always added new levels of complexity to that task. More than one thousand years ago human linkages began to assume continental proportions, but war and disease—a biological consequence of greater human interconnectedness—swept large parts of the Afro-Eurasian continent and delayed their global reach until the sixteenth century.

Thus the first wave of globalization assumed a very different form than a reading of human history one thousand years ago might have presumed. Weakened by plague and distracted by the activities of Eurasian warlords China never fulfilled the promise its economically powerful Song dynasty initially presented. Into the vacuum stepped a small number of European states whose fractious competitiveness provided motivation and whose accidental discovery of the Americas and its wealth provided both the means to insert themselves into the lucrative intra-Asian trade and the basis for a new Atlantic economy.

The first wave of globalization has often been interpreted as the consequence of European exceptionalism. But its cause lay instead in the sudden wealth Atlantic and Asian trade networks generated for many European countries. The ruling classes of the first wave's early protagonists—Spain, for example—tried to convert their newfound wealth into the basis for hegemony within Europe; in the end power flowed instead to societies like England and Holland that gave space to classes that generated wealth rather than plunder.

From the late sixteenth century onward commerce deepened the democratic imperative and in some communities made old forms of exclusion less viable, one reason later analysts gave centrality to capitalism as the motor for change. But it is the wider significance of the first wave in generating a process of democratization that should hold our attention.

We should also note that the first wave encompassed more than just Europe; it was of global significance. Although less all-embracing than subsequent waves, it radically altered global dynamics. For the first time some humans operated globally. They transformed intersecting regional markets into global networks and either directly or indirectly accelerated the global distribution of plants and animals, thereby spawning rapid population growth and altering environments. These changes had far-reaching political, social, and economic outcomes. For all societies the first wave of globalization was highly destabilizing.

In leading commercial nations such as England democratic changes in class relations and property laws further stimulated commercial activity, but they also increased the potential for social conflict. Commercial classes increased in size and influence. Urbanization expanded. Rural communities similarly changed as commercial activities increased. The interests of old elites were threatened. How those changes were managed not only dictated the success or otherwise of commercial activities but also determined the future character of societies. During the course of the seventeenth and eighteenth centuries many European societies sought stability through exclusions of class, religion, race, empire, or commercial monopoly. But their quests were never easy, and frequently countries turned to war and conquest as solutions. France did both at the end of the eighteenth century with consequences that were never nationally bounded.

Despite the instability generated by this nascent democratic imperative, the first wave's synergies also enabled a remarkable technological transformation that became the defining feature of the second wave. We have not always viewed industrialization as a consequence of globalization. Normally we portray it as an example of European or British exceptionalism, perhaps even as a product of the Enlightenment. Rarely is it presented as the remarkable outcome of global production and trade in commodities such as cotton, not to mention democratization.

However there can be no doubting the impact of industrialization. It enabled environments to carry larger populations, which in turn generated new social and political dynamics. More than ever before technology now had the capacity to generate huge profits. It also increased interconnectedness, enabling its own more rapid diffusion. Little wonder that so many writers give centrality to the role technology played in stimulating change. It altered the way humans produced, and it transformed the nature of their societies. But such writers often overlook a very important fact: what enabled the industrial entrance to resonate so rapidly and globally was human interconnectedness.

The initial beneficiaries of industrialization were societies whose elites had been transformed and expanded by the first wave of globalization. The Industrial Revolution was the payoff for enabling more people to participate in diverse and dynamic economic activities. That democratizing process continued during the nineteenth century and heralded a new age of the masses. A very different fate awaited societies unable to refashion themselves as industrial nations during the nineteenth century; they became imprisoned as colonies or semi-colonies in the industrial futures of other nations.

Yet national autonomy bestowed no security on industrializing countries. Perceptions of difference and rising anxieties over the internal tensions generated by industrial transformation soon tempted leaders to boost security and well-being by exclusionary tactics. In doing so, however. most national leaders failed to grasp that security and well-being came from economic and political empowerment, not conquest.

This meant that state systems had now to be more coherent and responsive; they had to be less hierarchical and autonomous than before. States had to make huge investments in communications infrastructure and human capital, the latter on a scale and depth never before envisaged by human communities. Such democratization threatened the power old elites enjoyed. They tried to slow down the impact of democratization. Some sought colonial successes to distract disaffected subjects. Japan turned to empire to offset the consequences of unequal development at home and competition abroad. The United States sought empire to symbolize its great power status, gain access to new wealth abroad, and bestow universally the benefits its leaders believed Social Darwinism had made possible at home. Not to be outdone Russia expanded eastward across Eurasia.

There were many other reasons for colonies: they sustained national confidence, they possessed strategic value, they restored competitive advantage, and they demonstrated global reach. But they brought no lasting stability. Empires created new forms of difference and inequality that denied colonial peoples the keys to successful transformation: autonomy and popular empowerment. Colonies involved zero-sum strategies. They destabilized communities. They denied inclusion. They suppressed demand. Industrial colonizers were blind to these consequences of their actions.

The second wave's collapse into world war and depression demonstrated the dangers exclusivity and monopolization carry. Instead of mechanisms for global cooperation and development the second wave witnessed nationalism and the creation of national empires that sought to become worlds unto themselves. Governing elites deluded themselves that they could control the multiple transformations and attendant conflicts rippling through their societies. Indeed with competition increasingly drawn in Darwinian terms they were prepared to go to the brink of war and beyond in order to gain hegemonic status at home and abroad. Of course they failed, and World War I cost their nations tremendously and not only in lives. It cost them the confidence that once energized the second wave of globalization.

Economic collapse generated a brutal depression within a decade of the war's end. The resulting inward-looking economic policies that almost all

industrial nations adopted simply reinforced the drive to empire and conquest that had already exacted a high price. During the 1930s and 1940s they
provoked a second round of blood-letting. Nothing better demonstrated the
futility of fostering zero-sum perceptions and of denying the democratic synergies that globalization gave space to than the avenging fascist conquerors
who believed that national solutions could come only from baptisms of fire
and empire.

Democracy and Globalization

A third wave of globalization soon followed the second wave's implosion in
the 1930s. War conferred on the United States unprecedented opportunity to
establish the first global world order. Indeed American globalism did generate a qualitatively different wave. It laid the basis for both domestic political
stability in industrialized nations and international cooperation. Through
state planning and social engineering it facilitated economic recovery for
its former industrial rivals. It also created new multilateral institutions to
manage international trade liberalization and prevent the return of ruinous
national economic competition. Both projects incorporated United States'
desires to maintain its hegemony, but in a more globalized world such desires
were not always possible to maintain.

American globalism also created an international environment in which
the second wave's empires of disadvantage could be dissolved. Thus decolonization, too, became a child of globalization and its struggles, although not
the uncontested Western gift it is still sometimes presented as. Of course
decolonization alone could not guarantee future meaningful participation in
the globalized economy for members of the emergent Third World. Nonetheless it did represent a break with the past and held the promise of autonomy
for societies that decolonized. But autonomy alone was never enough.

Colonialism left most independent countries poorly equipped to survive
in a more globalized world. In addition residues of the colonial past lingered
in the modernization policies that more-powerful industrial nations imposed as a condition for development assistance. They lingered also in the
perceptions people held of globalization at a time when the term was barely
recognized. Neither gave weight to the democratic imperative. Instead they
encouraged the segregation of economic sectors, denied social reform, and
reinforced dependence on export production. Consequently the promise of
decolonization was not always realized. Dictatorships flourished. Development faltered. Neocolonialism prospered. A democratic global divide emerged that still holds the potential to destabilize the third wave.

Residues of the past also lingered in the war of globalisms that erupted between the two victors of World War II, the United States and the Russian-dominated Union of Soviet Socialist Republics. Instead of peace and global harmony, the third wave began with a new global ideological division, an unprecedented arms race, and a destructive Soviet-American rivalry that spilled over into Eastern European occupations and Third World wars. It was not an auspicious start. In the end both globalisms died, one more dramatically than the other.

The victor was corporate transnationalism. When postwar prosperity ended in the 1970s, large corporations and their allies exploited popular fears of recession to deregulate domestic economies and transform global regulatory systems to their advantage. As transnational capital became more active, it harnessed a third generation of technological change to fashion global production networks. These networks often exploited Third World vulnerabilities, but their primary purpose was to promote corporate survival and find new avenues for profit.

By the close of the twentieth century corporate globalism held center stage and appeared to challenge many of the third wave's social achievements. Democratization had created wealthier, more-educated, and longer-living populations able to connect with industry in new and innovative ways. Its emphasis on equal opportunity and human rights spawned large urban civil communities with common interests and the capability of communicating with each other globally. Civil societies represented the symbiosis between economic growth and democratization. Transnationalism now appeared to threaten the gains many civil societies had won and perhaps also the social stability and harmony that had generated so much dynamism and creativity.

Indeed the whole rhetoric of postwar modernity derived directly from the shock waves of unprecedented empowerment that had rippled through industrialized societies after the mid-twentieth century. These shock waves reached deep into societies to transform working and domestic lives, family and social relationships, and gender and race relations. In countries like Italy and Japan, for example, change derived in part from a new willingness by industry and commerce to satisfy popular demands for inexpensive consumer goods that improved the quality of life. Both countries drew on strong craft traditions, but in the immediate postwar era a new focus on human capital transformed these societies into prosperous and creative powerhouses for lifestyle industries.

Such transformations, although uneven and often incomplete, demonstrated the possibilities democratization offered. They indicated also the dynamic character of the third wave, in particular its ability to generate among people new ways of thinking and new forms of action quite independent of the more hegemonic tendencies exhibited by American, Soviet, and corporate globalisms. We might call it the people's globalism, but in many respects it represents the same democratizing outcome that greater human interconnectedness—especially on a global scale—has always permitted by expanding the environments in which humans operate.

New Global Challenges

These new synergies demand from us new globalizing perspectives. The dynamics of globalization have changed, but the dangers they present are not dissimilar to those of the late eighteenth century or the early twentieth century. The third wave could falter; it could collapse.

Three challenges stand out. First the challenge of extending and deepening democratization globally and enhancing the centrality of civil society at a time when the attempted privatization of the third wave has strengthened short-term profit-maximizing strategies and forms of monopoly control at the expense of investment in human capital and infrastructure. The resulting increase in inequalities, exacerbated by war and debt, has cost the third wave much of its former legitimacy. The rise in inequalities has also increased the scope for corruption and for new policies of exclusion at a time when human expectations for empowerment have never been higher. Like the empires of old the First World, the industrialized world, cannot survive as a world unto itself. Human interconnectedness makes that impossible.

Second there is the environmental challenge of addressing issues of sustainability. Just as democracy cannot survive in a sea of poverty, so it cannot survive in an environmentally damaged and disease-ridden world. Economic behavior, in particular the drive for short-term profits, is not helpful in this regard. It contributes to many environmental and health disasters. So, too, do state quests for industrial might and big power status. But the challenges are much deeper than these two institutional responses suggest. Because environmental problems are also both cumulative and global, they can only be addressed by cooperative global strategies that employ technology in environmentally sensitive ways. The machinery for developing and implementing such strategies barely exists.

The third challenge concerns the tension between homogeneous national identities and the global dynamic of human diversity. In an age in which human strategies for security and well-being still include human migration, albeit on a scale that is both greater and more rapid than at any time in the past, all forms of exclusivity—especially national forms of identity—are unsustainable and can generate instability.

All three challenges represent divides that have the potential to cripple globalization and its human dynamic. Global institutions already exist that can help transform the third wave to meet these challenges. New ones can be created. But to develop frameworks for future growth and change requires that we enhance our global consciousness.

The key lies in continued democratization. Empowerment transforms class structures. It reduces barriers and broadens the scope for wealth generation. It encourages equity and the devolution of authority. It creates skills to manage complex societies and makes possible diverse solutions and new ways of understanding ourselves. But empowerment also requires consciousness of our global history and an understanding that our very basic human drives require equally basic material solutions. Accordingly our nascent global consciousness needs to be harnessed in material and institutional ways that can manage the human condition more positively and effect global solutions based on an inclusive rather than exclusive reading of human history.

PART 3

Western Civilization Reconsidered

Western Civilization and Its Discontents

Hanna H. Gray

I recently read the symposia held on the fate of the Western Civilization course published in the *History Teacher* in 1977 and in the *American Historical Review* in 1982. My conclusion: *plus ça change*. Debates over teaching the history of Western Civilization have been with us for decades. Nor will they go away.

These debates raise some quite different if related topics. One is curricular, having to do with conceptions of an ideal education, what education is for, what it is about, and how it should be organized and presented. Another concerns the problem of how history should be taught and where it fits into an essential program of a liberal education. Yet another relates to the definitions attached to the terms *Western* and *civilization*. How are the Western tradition and its history to be understood? Can one legitimately identify a major or dominant narrative and theme or set of themes to frame a coherent history that will introduce nonhistorians as well as future history concentrators to some basic knowledge and some sense of what it is to think historically? Or is the whole idea flawed in and of itself? Has it and does it inevitably lead to a parochial or triumphalist view of the West that subordinates the rest of the world and its culture to its perceived superiority, that interprets history in terms of a progressive development toward certain goals assumed to be of ultimate value while ignoring the achievements—even the contributions made to Western thought and institutions—of other cultures? Are such courses inevitably tainted by their own historical origins (for example, as is sometimes alleged, by the motives pertinent to two post-war moments that were expressed in the rhetoric of those who founded Columbia's Contemporary Civilization or in Harvard's "Red Book")?

From *Historically Speaking* 7 (September/October 2005).

Questions as to whether courses in the history of Western Civilization were simply outmoded or so seriously biased in their assumptions as to be dangerously useless were already current several decades ago. Support for their continuation has fluctuated among both students and faculty, with shifting perceptions of the priorities that liberal education should emphasize, conflicting opinions as to how to realize those in terms of pedagogic method, multiple views of history and even of its knowability, of what in history is most worth studying and how. And, of course, the work of historians and therefore the kind of history historians think important to convey to students have developed in all kinds of ways, in content, approach, and interdisciplinary styles. Above all there is the issue of whether it is oppressively artificial to study Western, as opposed to world or comparative history.

This is surely not the place to rehearse the arguments or review the many kinds of courses spawned by the disputes over core curricula and their alternatives. In fact most of the alternatives to general education or core curricula do have at least some requirements, however lightly imposed through distribution, and even existing core curricula are full of options for fulfilling the requirements they set. A very few colleges do continue to put all students through the same courses, but these in turn usually offer some variants within a common framework. Properly speaking there no longer exists such a thing as a single required course in the history of Western Civilization. If that *is* mandated, it is as a prerequisite for some special program and group of students.

In the meantime courses in the history of civilization have come widely to be seen as more or less fungible, with all civilizations regarded as equal. In my own university, for example, (and, I have to admit, rather to my distress) students now have a requirement called "civilization studies" that extends to a choice among ancient, European, Judaic, Russian, African, Latin American, South Asian, East Asian, and other variants. Each sequence, according to the catalogue, "provides an in-depth examination of one of the world's great civilizations through direct encounters with some of its most significant documents and monuments." Nor is the civilization-studies requirement designed necessarily as an introduction to history, although it may well be taught that way.

The University of Chicago's current curriculum is obviously only one option among many for dealing with the quandary that has long since overtaken those engaged with the problem of structuring a liberal education in a world seen to have far too many subjects worth studying and for a world where internationalism, pluralism, and rapid change are seen as the driving realities for which students are to be prepared. For some the answer lies in turning to world history or comparative history as an introductory course. For others it has to do with providing courses of different types that demonstrate what historians actually do on an intensive rather than survey scale. And for still others the solution is to reanimate the Western Civilization course in a way that takes full account of the objections to some of its surrounding traditions and that opens a path to the study of other cultures as well.

In my ideal college students would have to take Western Civilization and then either a non-Western course or one dealing with comparative or world history. In my view they need both. But given the symbolism that has come to be accorded Western Civilization and its discontents, my course probably needs a new name.

Courses in Western Civilization, as opposed to introductory courses in European history, have tended to concentrate in some form on the historical interaction between ideas and institutional developments. They have usually focused on critical moments of change or revolution, transitions from one basic mode of thought to another, or differing responses to and interpretations of large questions having to do with the nature of the political and social order. They have tried to shake students loose from accepted opinions and unthinking assumptions and encourage critical analysis and independent judgment. Some courses have placed emphasis on change in history, others on problems that recur over different eras, others on thinking about history as an intellectual discipline. Whatever their principal purposes these courses have been founded in some conviction that the condition we inhabit is the product of a historical process that has created a distinctive culture and common inheritance whose features are written in our own history even as they continue to evolve.

Against such traditional views are raised the voices that point to the global character of our world and the need to see the West in a much-larger frame. Other voices point out that the kind of history represented in the traditional course tends to ignore the "newer" history, especially social history, and to glide over the unchanging or slowly changing phenomena of the past, as well as to ignore newer approaches to and methods of historical scholarship. And then there are voices that detect a political or ideological defect in the underlying justification for the kind of material presented. The charge may have to do with "Eurocentrism" or with "elitism" or with a failure to acknowledge the claims of women or minorities or the nameless in the human story or with a presumption that history operates from above and constitutes a story of progress to ends that represent the interests of the powerful and a modernity whose values, it is claimed, are incorporated as unchallenged. Such are some of the arguments against the required course in the history of Western Civilization.

It seems to me that one can only do so much at one time. Further it is important first to understand something about one's own culture before one can gain more clearly from the study of others. Also we in the West do share a common inheritance, however differently we come to it and however selectively we engage it. And it is woven into the fabric of our institutions, language, outlook, experience, and practice in ways that we need to recognize and examine for ourselves. In the unusually terse words of Cicero "Not to know what came before you is to remain always a child."

I would still hope that a large portion of any course in the history of Western Civilization be based on important texts and on some of the seminal ideas that characterize this culture. Not because that is the only history. In a sense I am advocating a kind of historically shaped and humanistically oriented course of a sort that I think basic to a serious program in the liberal arts. I do not believe that this "privileges" Western history above other histories or asserts a stance of moral superiority.

I do not for a moment believe that to offer Western Civilization implies the belief that this culture dominates the world or that it means adherence to one narrative, one group, or one way of thought. I do not think that to study the elite is "elitist" or to study the underrepresented is to be "democratic." I cannot imagine that Western Civilization is rendered valueless because the motives of inculcating patriotism or civic virtue might have moved some of its supporters at various times. I don't for an instant believe that innocent minds will be brainwashed and led astray to celebrate the prejudices of Western hegemony. In short I agree with Irving Howe's point that because there is a political dimension in just about anything, not everything is political.[1]

The history of Western culture, from the ancients on, has been a history of criticism and debate, of constant questioning and skeptical analysis. Indeed Western culture is founded on a long tradition of self-criticism, one ultimately deepened through its discoveries of other cultures as well. A course in the history of Western Civilization ought at its best to introduce the ongoing debate over the questions that lie at the heart of this tradition. And our course will inevitably be attending also to significant European encounters with other cultures. More space than might once have been allotted can and should be devoted to both sides of these phenomena and their effects.

It may be worth recalling some more words of that old-fashioned radical Howe as he looked back on his experience of liberal education at CCNY [City College of New York]:

Knowledge of the past, we felt, could humanize by promoting distance from ourselves and our narrow habits, and this could promote critical thought. Even partly to grasp a significant experience or literary work of the past would require historical imagination, a sense of other times, which entailed moral imagination, a sense of other ways. It would create a kinship with those who had come before us, hoping and suffering as we have, seeking through language, sound, and color to leave behind something of enduring value.[2]

American culture is notorious for its indifference to the past. . . . But the past is the substance out of which the present has been formed, and to let it slip away from us is to acquiesce in the thinness that characterizes so much of our culture. Serious education must assume, in part, an adversarial stance toward the very society that sustains it—a democratic society makes the wager that it's worth supporting a culture of criticism. But if that criticism loses touch with the heritage of the past, it becomes weightless, a mere compendium of momentary complaints.[3]

Not to be educated in the cultural inheritance of one's own society is to be seriously uneducated. But not to understand the limitations of that inheritance—not to have come to realize that some understanding of Western Civilization is only the beginning and not the end of education—would be to remain uneducated.

NOTES

1. Irving Howe, "The Value of the Canon," in *Debating P.C.,* ed. Paul Berman (New York: Dell, 1992), 153–71.
2. Ibid., 159.
3. Ibid., 162.

Western Civ and World History

Conflicts and Complements

Peter N. Stearns

Anyone conversant with the history teaching scene in the United States over the past twenty years knows about the running battle between Western Civ and world history as foci for survey courses served up to college freshmen and not a few high-school students. The conflict has several fronts. Coverage competition looms large. It is impossible to do justice to the standard topics of a Western Civ course and the ambitious canons of a world history course in the same year. A common effort at compromise, the high-school world-history course (usually tenth grade) that is in fact 67 percent Western, is legitimately ridiculed by world historians as providing a civilizationally skewed vision of what the world was and is all about.

Competition over values is at least as fierce and ultimately more intractable. While some partisans of Western Civilization courses are primarily attracted by the comforts of routine and familiarity, others, including a number of political and educational leaders, see in the course a defense of superior traditions in an uncertain world, an opportunity to preach unified values to an increasingly diverse American student population. Thus the 99-1 United States Senate vote against the world-history portion of the "history standards" issued in 1992, which insisted that any educational recipients of federal money should have a "decent respect for the values of Western civilization." Thus second lady Lynne Cheney's assertion that 9/11—a tragedy that seemed to many a call for greater understanding of the world at large—showed how essential it was to rally around Western values and a Western curriculum. World history partisans, in some instances, have replied in kind

From *Historically Speaking* 5 (March 2004).

with a gleeful effort at West bashing and (as critics rightly pointed out in the history standards debate) a virtuous attempt to shield other civilizations from adverse comment.

This aspect of the conflict reflects the resurgence of cultural conservatism in the United States, but it also picks up on the history of the Western Civ course itself. The course was designed in the early decades of the twentieth century by American educators eager to demonstrate the deeper roots of their own upstart society—in another period of rapid immigration—but also concerned about diplomatic instability following World War I. As one partisan put it, the Western Civ course was designed to help students make a choice between "utopia and barbarism." In this vein innovators conceived of Western Civ as, effectively, the only civilizational tradition, with a straight line from ancient Egypt and Mesopotamia to the glories of Anglo-American constitutionalism. They saw their course as a mixture of triumphant coverage and an inculcation of precious but now threatened values. World historians, by no means uniform West bashers, simply have to dissent from this tradition. Their vision must encompass a number of different civilizations (or larger world forces that downplay civilizations altogether) and their values, implicitly emphasizing cosmopolitanism and tolerance, point in an alternate direction as well.

In practice, to be sure, the battle has not raged as bitterly as periodic rhetoric might imply. In the advanced-placement arena, both world-history and European-history programs are flourishing (the former is gaining ground, in part because its recent emergence leaves more room for growth). Colleges and universities differ in their choices for survey courses, and some programs, as at Stanford, have combined a traditional Western requirement with imaginative comparative offerings. The idea of sequences of courses, as a logical solution to the dilemma of choice, has not penetrated very far, because the American educational system is so resolutely chaotic where history is concerned and because partisans are unwilling to yield terrain at any particular point. It would be possible, for example, to see high schools as offering a civilizational approach followed by college-level world history or vice versa, but that assumes a level of coordination that simply does not exist in the United States, as well as a willingness of, say, world historians to abandon high school in favor of college (or Western Civists to cede college), which so far has proved to be too much to ask. But pure Western Civ is on the decline—most state requirements insist on some world coverage, though often in Western-oriented amalgams that displease world-history purists—and a continued evolution toward a greater awareness of global history is likely.

Yet one crucial aspect of the tension between world history and Western Civ has not been adequately explored, if only because Western Civ advocates fear any concession, while world historians are often too busy figuring out how to downplay or readjust the West to give serious thought to more imaginative amalgams. Consider the following solution. The West should be viewed as one civilization among several, rather than the whole show. At the same time the West should be granted analytical significance that goes beyond either debunking or rueful acknowledgments of modern power. Now a series of interesting opportunities arises, which permit efforts to interpret the Western tradition within a legitimate world-history framework.

The key is comparison, a standard world-history tool that now needs to be deployed in the Western Civ arena as well. What, in fact, are the major distinctive features in Western institutions and values as the civilization has unfolded across many centuries? The question is oddly unasked; particularly in Western Civ courses themselves but also in many world-history surveys. Partly it goes unasked because we have become accustomed to a factual narrative, a set of historical stories, that pass for conveying what Western civilization is all about (the same turgidness can creep into the coverage of other civilizations in world history, but it is less prominent if only because the civilizational traditions are less deeply established in our teaching conventions). And if, in the more specific Western Civ tradition, we assume that Western is both distinctive and better by definition, the need for explicit comparison is simply bypassed. Putting the same point another way: the Western Civ teaching tradition has always been implicitly comparative—the Western story is older and better—but rarely explicitly so. Analytical linkage between Western Civ and world history depends on bringing latent assumptions out for focused examination.

Comparison, in turn, yields a number of ensuing questions. When, first of all, did Western civilization begin? The Western Civ tradition assumes the answer is coincident with the emergence of civilization itself, but in fact this is hard to sustain when Western civilization is handled with the same inquiry about origins that would apply to Indian, Chinese, or Middle Eastern civilizations. Western Civ courses, as they have turned into more-standard survey narratives, have often shortened the timespan involved, beginning with Greece and Rome, or the Middle Ages, or even later. But they, too, have usually ducked explicit inquiry into when the West actually begins, because dealing with these issues assumes a capacity to define a distinctive Westernness. Talking directly with students about the classical versus medieval options (both can be defended, depending on what aspects of the Western tradition seem crucial) is an initial way of putting Western civilization in a framework compatible with the treatment of other civilizations and therefore with world history.

After origins one moves to key changes in the Western tradition, to the principal periodization of Western history evaluated in comparative context. William H. McNeill once argued that the West has changed more than other major civilizations. I'm not sure this is a defendable proposition (here, too, explicit comparison would be revealing). But certainly in the early modern period the claim applies, and this raises the issue of what remains Western even amid rapid change and also how the definition of a distinctive Westerness evolves as well. In dealing with change a focus not only on familiar topics, like the parliamentary tradition, but also on other key areas where Westerness may apply, like gender relations, will greatly improve the analysis.

By the early modern period as well the question of *where* Western Civ was and is gets added to issues of effective origins and major change. Like many civilizations the West has had a shifting geography, and it has generated borderlands or zones of unusual contact where issues of inclusion or differentiation simply cannot be avoided. (Similar issues apply to East Asian civilization —is it a whole, or must it be divided among China, Japan, Korea, and so on?) For the West connections to Eastern and Central Europe (being redefined in the contemporary world once again) and even to Russia and also to the Americas and Austria / New Zealand require explicit analysis that in turn will enhance the capacity to discuss what the essentials of the Western tradition "really" are. That the same discussion requires teachers and students to confront some "exceptionalist" claims, particularly for the United States, adds to the challenge but also, ultimately, to the potential for integration.

From the late nineteenth century onward questions two and three (capturing change within the Western tradition and dealing with shifting geography) are further refined by the need to deal with the considerable Westernization of other parts of the world—Japan being a leading case in point. As other societies successfully incorporate industrialization, consumer culture, and parliamentary democracy, does a definably distinctive West remain? Here again is a compelling focus both for the later stages of a Western Civ course, taught in world-history context, and for dealing with one major case of a larger question about homogenization and differentiation in closing out a world-history survey.

Comparison is the most obvious way to move from assumptions in the Western Civ tradition to the kind of discussion that is compatible with world history, but there are other bridges as well. Along with comparison intersocietal contact is a key technique in world history. Elements of the Western Civ tradition have, of course, long stressed contact—the kind that emanated from the West from the early modern period onward. A world-history approach must incorporate Western-generated contacts, but it adds two points to the analysis. First it urges a closer look at the West as a recipient of influences from other societies—not a brand-new topic but underexplored in the more-triumphal versions of the Western Civ tradition. This means, particularly, lots of attention to the West as an imitative society in the postclassical (medieval) period—where, in fact, comparisons with other imitators, like Japan or sub-Saharan Africa, are quite revealing. The second addition, here particularly for more-modern times, involves the realization that contacts are complex, that what the West sent out from the sixteenth century onward, from Christianity to consumerism, gets variously interpreted and syncretically combined, a process very much still going forward.

It goes without saying that a more analytical approach to Western civilization, derived from a world-history context, embraces both thorns and roses. Some relatively distinctive features of the Western tradition will seem positive (particularly because we inevitably evaluate under some influence from this same tradition), but others, like a willingness to enslave or the modern Western penchant for racism, are more troubling. Comparison can serve neither triumphalism nor West bashing entirely.

The analytical issues evoked in this sketch are complex and designed for debate. They do not resolve agonizing practical issues of competing coverage. But comparative analysis can cut through some of the often-sterile debate between the two survey options. Certainly students in a Western Civ course that looks to other societies for measurements of Western distinctiveness and is open to the importance and complexity of contacts will have an easier time moving into a world-history program, should some sequencing be possible. A Western-oriented world-history course, though still potentially misleading, becomes less objectionable if analytically sharpened. Above all a willingness to deal seriously with the Western tradition—but with more-explicit analytical tools—improves the possibility of incorporating Western history into a world-history program. Even coverage decisions are improved through a willingness to focus on comparative essentials. To be sure the compromise is slanted to the world-history side, though it builds on assumptions that need to be tested within the Western Civ tradition itself. But the capacity to find the West in world history (along, of course, with other major traditions; that's the whole basis for comparison) should facilitate more-constructive conversation among two still-hostile camps.

Western Exceptionalism and Universality Revisited

John M. Headley

A mong the big losers in the historiography of the last several decades are the dignity of Western civilization, the centrality of political history, and the earlier assessment of the nature and virtues of the Renaissance. Although much has been accomplished to extend the variety, ambiguity, and inclusiveness of history, the most obvious casualties are: the notion of Western exceptionalism and universality, contemned; the importance of political history, marginalized, even extinguished; and the Renaissance, reduced, if not abolished. If we wish to propose the recentering of the West in the present discussion, the related issues of the deliberate neglect of political history and the undermining of the Renaissance as a concept are intimately involved and constitute an integral part of our argument.

It has become fashionable to heap condemnation and blame upon the career of Western civilization, rejecting or denying its claims to uniqueness, exceptionalism, and universality, despite the historical record to the contrary. This record is seen most immediately in the early definition and distinguishing of the secular from the priestly or ecclesiastical, evident in Augustine and in Pope Gelasius I's pronouncement of 494, which served to distinguish the authority of the moral and religious from the powers of the political; second, more practically and less theoretically, in the competitive rather than unitary structure of the European experience, dictated by the distinctive topography of the westernmost peninsula of Eurasia and the variety of migrating peoples invading the Roman Empire; and finally in the twin universalisms of the Stoic-Christian amalgam at the beginning of the Christian Common Era. Only Islam could contest this last, the uniqueness of Western universalism;

From *Historically Speaking* 9 (November/December 2007).

whatever its better record of toleration through *dhimmi,* the recognition of protected peoples of the book, Islam in its proselytizing approached the world not as did Christianity, as a single parish, but as something fractured from the outset between the House of Islam and the House of War. Thus inclusion in the *umma,* the whole Islamic community, involved not only the overcoming of a most essential, almost ontological, rift in the diaspora of humankind but also the admitting of a high degree of necessary violence, intrinsic to the life and experience of its founder.

On the basis of impact and influence rather than origins Western exceptionalism and universality are normally argued as being limited to an essentially unquestioned achievement in science and technology by which the modern world continues to be influenced. Here the social philosopher Ernest Gellner claims for the West a "culture-transcending" capacity.[1] But the same can be claimed, although indeed less obviously, for two political—legal and constitutional—developments of the West: the idea of a common humanity, generating programs of human rights; and the admission of political dissent, which contrasts with practices everywhere else that pursue prompt exclusion through prison, exile, or extermination. Over the past several decades the very neglect of political history has served to obscure the uniqueness of the Western political accomplishment in these two respects.

Although the second of these developments will not be considered here, both are properly political and have been operative since the late eighteenth century. Nevertheless their historical importance and vitality have been displaced by new fashions, interests, and orthodoxies—some of them quite sound and justifiable for history and the social sciences, such as addressing the new frontier of global processes or globalization. And while our hands are groping amid the trash heap to recover the notion of Western universality and the long-extracted central axis of politics to history, almost inevitably we manage to bring within our grasp the Renaissance in its fragile remains, increasingly cannibalized by university administrators, who struggle to meet —along with other less-worthy claims—the expanding demands and valid needs in the field of world or global history. From this awkward, even precarious posture of overstretch our present task comes into focus: with an expanded and reconstituted view of the Renaissance as the veritable fulcrum of intellectual leverage, we will argue for the West's universalizing reach in aspiring to the unity of mankind.

Possibly the single most important recovery from the ruins of the classical world is the thoroughly Renaissance humanistic event of the translation from Greek into Latin of Claudius Ptolemy's *Geographia,* first published in

1475 and printed with maps repeatedly thereafter. This event profoundly reflected what we have come to expect of humanism and the Renaissance: it occurred within the circle of young aficionados of the study of classical Greek, created by the distinguished diplomat and teacher Manuel Chrysoloras in Florence at the end of the fourteenth century. In the *Geographia* Ptolemy defines his subject "as a survey of the earth in its just proportions," and he calls upon its practitioners "to concentrate upon position rather than the quality [that is, nature] of a place."[2] It can well be judged the most significant single work among the classical texts recovered by the Italian Renaissance, for it beckoned artists and astronomers, cartographers and navigators to apply a mathematical proportionality to the visible world.

Ptolemy cast over the Earth's known inhabited surface, the *oikoumene,* a net of mathematical coordinates, or graticule—the latitude and longitude of the Alexandrian school—whereby he could presumably establish with mathematical exactitude the location of individual places. The assumption that permitted such mathematization arose from the confidence that the Earth's surface was essentially homogeneous. The resulting grid not only came to be extended globally to an expanded ecumene but was increasingly refined and tightened to become another metaphor for human existence in the dawning modern age.

A continuously refined and more sophisticated Renaissance cartography, along with improved navigation, made possible European expansion and the Age of Discovery. Geography as a distinct form of knowledge and the geographical culture of sixteenth-century Renaissance Europe appear here not simply because the subject seems to have escaped the direct attention of historians in suggesting an expanded understanding of the Renaissance but also because of the specifically universalizing theme associated with the advancement of geography. No other intellectual discipline serves the total comprehensive aspirations, whether exploitative or missionary, of a civilization as does geography. In its immediate address to the lands and peoples of the Earth, when associated with the improved technology of sixteenth-century navigation, geographic knowledge brought the entire globe within the emerging discipline's survey and eventual compass. The result served to establish the specifically universalizing character of geography as a new knowledge that could be exploited for religious, political, economic, and military purposes upon a global stage.

At midcentury Venice constituted the cartographic center of Europe. The cosmographer to the republic, Giacomo Gastaldi, surpassed all others, and his friend Giovanni Battista Ramusio, through his *Navigazioni e viaggi,* committed himself to what amounted to establishing the globe's habitability and potential communicability—a view of the entire Earth that broke with and junked the traditional picture left by the second-century B.C.E. Stoic philosopher and librarian Crates of Mallos, which presented the planet as made up of four noncommunicating yet inhabited continents. Ramusio's travel accounts, together with his own supporting arguments, trumpeted the Earth's total habitability, manifested empirically in the course of the late Renaissance—the sixteenth century—by Europe's engagement of the Earth's peoples.[3] The new, very recent interconnectedness of the Earth's peoples achieved by superior European cartography and navigation but significantly sustained henceforth by sea power made possible the permanent settlement, expanding colonialism, empires, and, yes, slavery and exploitation that mark the creation of the Atlantic world. Europe's precarious toeholds in Asia had to await the late eighteenth century to be expanded into comparable colonial empires. What is important here is that these new links of global intercon-nectedness of the Earth's peoples allow the Renaissance, through its unique experience and achievement, to be seen not as a university administrator's throwaway but as the veritable portal to our own global age. Geography both as a discipline and as a culture must be effectively integrated with the Age of Exploration in order to reveal an expanded view of the European Renais-sance.

As used in this analysis the term *universal* connotes the principle inheri-ted from classical antiquity that expresses a potentially comprehensive inte-gration or inclusion of all peoples into a broad community, together with the legal and constitutional issues that this process entails. The expanding inhab-ited world or *oikoumene* of the Greek experience, informed by the Stoic notion of cosmopolis, found its practical realization in the Roman Empire and Roman law. Although Cicero defined the "barbarians" and the "provin-cials" apart from the resulting community, at the same time aspiring to their eventual inclusion, he extended to them that community. As one scholar expresses it, "The frontier between the world of civil men and that of the barbarians was forever dissolving." Christianity itself provided a further reinforcement and dimension to this universal dynamic, as evinced in the Pauline appeal to a transcendent oneness in Christ Jesus (Galatians 3:28). With the grafting of the Christian church onto the Roman community, the Imperium Christianum partook of and extended this same "simultaneous open exclusiveness," this tension between an apparently narrow identity and a potentially broad inclusion.[4] The Aristotelian-Ciceronian complex served to demarcate the world of civil (urban) civic humanity from the barbarians, provincials, *pagani,* and outsiders yet opened itself up to their inclusion. Both the fifth-century Christian and the sixteenth-century European, chiefly the Spaniard, had recourse to this complex mechanism of incorporation.

With the penetration and grafting of the new Christian faith onto the ultimate form of classical culture we have the supreme knitting together of the two great statements of human universality standing at the ground and the beginning of our civilization. The remarkable meshing of the universalism offered by Stoicism in its idea of cosmopolis with the complementary universalism of Christ's Body, however, never proved a perfect fit. Humanity, having been first identified with membership in the civil Roman community, after 380 C.E. was reinforced by association with the now-coercive Christian church. The ideals of civility, humanity, and Christianity moved together, simultaneously exclusive in defining the New Society but open-ended in extending the composite to the rest of humankind as worthy of inclusion in the club. This powerful principle of universal inclusion and incorporation emerged as the ancient world's greatest single legacy.

In the general recovery of Roman law, following the eleventh century, the church, which had fashioned itself as an ecclesiastical empire on the model of its Roman predecessor, was better equipped than any of the contemporary motley kingdoms not only to adopt this law for itself in an ecclesiastical rendering of imperial Roman law but also to create in canon law the "First Modern Western Legal System" common to all the Latin Christian political communities.[5] Thus we need to attend to the ruminations of the twelfth-century canonists on the various meanings of that fateful term *jus naturale,* or natural law.

Apart from the most immediate meaning of *jus naturale* as some absolute, higher law of what is right—moral, divine, or immanent in the universe— a more individual sense surfaced. The twelfth-century canonists began to be sensitive not merely to the just thing itself but to what was justly due someone. They defined *jus* in a subjective sense as a faculty, power, force, or ability pertaining inherently to individuals, and they then proceeded to develop a panoply of such apparently natural rights—among them the ownership of property and the capacity of individuals to form their own government. Thus an inhering universal claim promoted individual, particular expression. Pope Innocent IV in 1250 extended these two rights to infidels and Christians alike. In the course of the century other rights, such as the right to liberty and self-defense and the right of the poor to be safeguarded from hunger, came to be defined. The marvelous ambivalence of *jus* as meaning both a higher law and the inherent rights defined by that law began to resonate through the language of the Gregorian decretals and their medieval commentaries. This inheritance entered formal political philosophy with William of Ockham and by 1400 was recapitulated by Jean Gerson in his important definition of *jus* as "a power or faculty belonging to each one in accordance with the dictate of right reason."[6] The great Spanish juristic theologians of the sixteenth century would usher this rich tradition into the early modern period.

In 1539 the mid-thirteenth-century rulings of Innocent IV regarding the rights of infidels to the holding of property and to the determination of their own government were reaffirmed in the explosive context of the American Indians by the great Dominican Francisco de Vitoria: "Barbarians are not impeded from being true masters publicly and privately, either by mortal sin in general or by the particulars of unbelief."[7] The assertion was more than academic for Vitoria's fellow Dominican Bartolomé de Las Casas. Speaking from the political and evangelical trenches of engagement he resoundingly rebutted the Aristotelian humanist Juan Ginés de Sepúlveda's attitude toward the Indian: "They are our brothers, and Christ gave his life for them." Nor did he limit his outlook to the immediate problem represented by the Amerindian; in fact, he rose to a view that included blacks and Asians as well. Quoting Cicero and, significantly, appealing to the Stoic idea of a universal brotherhood of men, Las Casas insisted: "All the peoples of the world are humans and there is only one definition of all humans and of each one, that is, that are rational. . . . Thus all the races of humankind are one."[8] Yet despite these glorious instances of sustained continuance of a tradition that potentially directed itself to all humans a broader, more positive reading of natural law, opening that law up to all the peoples of the planet, survived rather than prevailed during the course of the sixteenth century.

This shedding of natural law's specifically religious framework, this secularization of the concept, would prove to be of decisive importance, for it made any program of human rights and the vision of a single humanity religiously neutral and hence potentially neutral with respect to culture, preparing the ground for its true universality. In the next century we encounter through Hugo Grotius and Thomas Hobbes the decisive secularization of natural law and its vital rerouting in preparation for its universalization and greater adaptability to an extra-Christian world. Although Grotius finds the common characteristic of all humans to be an impelling desire for society and that human nature itself is the mother of natural law, he does not divorce himself from all moral and religious principles so completely as to go down the route momentarily opened up by his great hypothesis—that natural law would persist even if there were no God.[9]

For his younger contemporary Hobbes, a more radical modernizer, self-preservation would resoundingly distinguish the new basis of natural right. Hobbes, of course, forsakes all metaphysical and ontological references to construct from a new and irreducible basis, found in "the Natural Condition of Mankind," the notorious "state of nature." Political existence was no longer natural but "artificial" and contractual. The hypothetical, precivil condition of man revealed a single right, uniformly present and common to all men—the right to self-preservation. Natural right comes to supplant natural law in the new environment of uniformity.[10] Hobbes's successors retained the vocabulary of natural law, but any sort of organic endowment of the notion of natural law was stripped away in the new world of rights in order to advance the abstraction of a basic equality inhering to the human condition. In the new context of seventeenth-century northern Europe, natural law and rights became transformed. Whatever transcendence natural law had seemed to possess in its capacity to obligate as well as to evoke universality appears to have been evacuated. These positions, insofar as they were recognized at all, came to be occupied by the more subjective view of natural law as common and universal to all humans. The fundamental unity of mankind in one common human nature became the prime consideration. The great legacy of our civilization appears to be less in its science and technology and more in the unifying force and challenge, the aspiration to a comprehensive political community, that cuts through the myriad instances of localism and tribalism cluttering the geodetic surface. It is this aspiration that had the capacity to transcend the culturally specific in the creation of a world citizenry, if not a world governance.

There is no need to rehearse the subsequent developments of John Locke and succeeding generations leading up to the age of democratic revolution, for that is a better-known story. The preceding five hundred years of statement and development, not as well known, concern us here, calling to account those who foreshorten history by beginning it too recently. Significantly Locke and his successors would speak with increasing frequency regarding mankind. In Edmund Burke's announcement regarding the unrolling of the "great map of mankind," late eighteenth-century Europe sought to acquire that picture of the degrees of barbarism and of refinement (that is, civilization) brought under a single gauge.[11] Unfortunately the notion of mankind served to draw with it the sinister typology of race and the Orwellian incongruity that while all are equal, some are more equal than others.

In the nineteenth century—the age of historicism, so much in conflict with the grand fictions of natural law but also an age of rising racial arrogance, the pride of great imperial systems, and the smoldering strain of national rivalries—reflection upon the natural rights of humans suffered an abeyance, remaining dormant yet operative. The violent divisiveness and particularism of race, nation, and social group turned Europe away from the currents of universality and its promise. In the subsequent century the League of Nations apparently saw no need to attempt some statement regarding natural rights. Not until the terrible yank into consciousness effected by World War II and its horrors did an expanded Western world, including now the better part of the globe, come to its senses largely through American initiative and leadership, resulting in 1948 in the Universal Declaration of Human Rights. Therein the natural rights "of men" become human rights in the express inclusion of the other half of humanity.

In conclusion our argument has sought to establish a tradition of fundamental thought and concern that stretches in its development from the initial Stoic-Christian statement through the Middle Ages to the present. No other civilization can mount such a case of sustained, continuous concern. Islam has its *shari'a,* whose own claims to universality will forever be hobbled by its being rooted in a specific religious confession and commitment.

Among all the great cultures and civilizations of the world there have been scattered moments of universality: India has not been without the tolerance manifested by the Emperor Akbar nor China without the compassion expressed by the Confucian Mencius. But the fragmentary and the occasional contrast starkly with the sustained and the continuous.

And yet there is no room for triumphalism in the painful progression of the West's ruminations upon the principles of equality, liberty, and effective justice. Whatever splendid ideals that have emerged have inevitably come wrapped in human failings and faults, delayed by human exploitation, greed, and shortsightedness. Nevertheless the intellectual machinery is there, as well as an essentially supportive, receptive context. If there is an apparently inexorable logic to the idea of equality once enunciated, it can be unnaturally stifled or delayed in its passage, promotion, and advance. Given the force and logic of the ideal, an immortal spur upon the conscience, death-transcendent, there is always someone—some person or fated generation—far down the track that actually takes the principle seriously, lifts it out of the mire, and is in a position to correct the injustice or move the process nearer to its logical, comprehensive inclusion. Thus would Abraham Lincoln take the necessary step that Jefferson found impossible to effect. Speaking prior to his presidency on the Dred Scott decision, Lincoln shone this light on the recurring dilemma:

I think the authors of that notable instrument [the Declaration of Independence] intended to include *all* men, but they did not intend to declare all men equal *in all respects.* . . . They did not mean to assert the obvious untruth that all were then actually enjoying that equality, nor yet that they were about to confer it immediately upon them. In fact, they had no power to confer such a boon. They meant simply to declare the right, so that the enforcement of it might follow as fast as circumstances should permit.[12]

Continuous? Perhaps not. But certainly sustained, ever resurgent, recoverable.

Notes

1. Ernest Gellner, *Postmodernism, Reason, and Religion* (London: Routledge, 1992), 71, 77–79.

2. Joan Gadol, *Leon Battista Alberti: Universal Man of the Early Renaissance* (Chicago: University of Chicago Press, 1969), 70–71, 198–200.

3. See my article "The Sixteenth-century Venetian Celebration of the Earth's Total Habitability: The Issue of the Fully Habitable World for Renaissance Europe," *Journal of World History* 8 (1997): 1–27.

4. Anthony Pagden, *Lords of all the World: Ideologies of Empire in Spain, Britain, and France c. 1500–c. 1800* (New Haven, Conn.: Yale University Press, 1995), 11–63; especially 21–24.

5. Harold Joseph Berman, *Law and Revolution: The Formation of the Western Legal Tradition* (Cambridge, Mass.: Harvard University Press, 1983), 199–254.

6. Brian Tierney, "Religious Rights: An Historical Perspective," in *Religious Human Rights in Global Perspective: Religious Perspectives,* ed. John Witte Jr. and John D. van der Vyver (The Hague: Martinus Nijhoff, 1996), 17–45, especially 28–29.

7. Francisco de Vitoria, *Political Writings,* ed. Anthony Pagden and Jeremy Lawrance (Cambridge, U.K.: Cambridge University Press, 1991), 246.

8. Brian Tierney, *The Idea of Natural Rights* (Grand Rapids, Mich.: Eerdmans, 1997), 273, 286–87.

9. Hugo Grotius, *Prolegomena to the Law of War and Peace* (New York: Library of Liberal Arts Press, 1957), sections 6, 16, and 11.

10. Thomas Hobbes, *Leviathan,* J. C. A. Gaskin ed. (Oxford: Oxford University Press), 1:13.

11. P. J. Marshall and Glyndwr Williams, *The Great Map of Mankind: Perceptions of New Worlds in the Age of Enlightenment* (Cambridge, Mass.: Harvard University Press, 1982), 1.

12. Abraham Lincoln, *The Speeches of Abraham Lincoln,* ed. Maureen Harrison and Steve Gilbert (San Diego, Calif.: Excellent, 2005), 40.

Recentering the West?

Constantin Fasolt

> MONSIEUR JOURDAIN: What! When I say, "Nicole, bring me my
> slippers, and give me my nightcap," that's prose?
> PHILOSOPHY MASTER: Yes, Sir.
> MONSIEUR JOURDAIN: By my faith! For more than forty years I have
> been speaking prose without knowing anything about it, and I am
> much obliged to you for having taught me that.

John Headley believes the West has been unfairly maligned. That is probably true. He speaks up for the dignity of Western civilization. Surely
Western civilization does deserve respect. He also worries about the lack
of attention paid to political history, and he stresses the importance of the
Renaissance. As someone who has tried to understand the ins and outs of
early modern European history, I share his regret over what strikes me as the
increasing speed with which the Renaissance, along with much other history
extending further back in time than the nineteenth century, seems to be
vanishing from the repertory of contemporary historians. He points to the
remarkable and insufficiently noticed role played by geography and cartography in Europe's understanding of humanity as global and in its conquest of
the globe inhabited by that humanity. He underlines the length and coherence of an intellectual tradition that extends from ancient Stoicism and
Christianity to modern theories of natural law and human rights, a tradition
that is sweeping the globe today and crucial to the legitimation of political
dissent. But Headley is by no means a triumphalist. His praise of the West is
tempered by his acknowledgment of slavery, colonialism, imperialism, and
other instances of Western greed and shortsightedness. But when everything

From *Historically Speaking* 9 (November/December 2007).

is said and done, he does insist that Western civilization deserves to be recognized for the unique and unrelenting universalism with which it made cultural and religious neutrality conceivable, and without which a common humanity would be impossible to imagine. He would like to restore the West to the central place in history to which he is convinced it is entitled.

Headley has my sympathy. But sympathy is hardly what he wants. He wants agreement with his case for recentering the West. And that, with all respect due to his scholarly integrity and candor and in spite of my agreement with many of the points he makes, I cannot really give. For the purposes of this response I shall state three different but related reasons for withholding my agreement.

One reason is that I cannot tell exactly what I am supposed to agree with. I find it difficult to understand what Headley means by Western exceptionalism. That the West is different from all other civilizations is easy enough to grant because it is so obviously true. But the same is true of all other civilizations: each is different from all others, including the West. Indeed it is obviously true of everything to which we care to give a name: Tom is unique, and so is Dick, not to mention Harry. It may therefore well be that Western Harry puts a higher premium on religious neutrality than Oriental Tom. But that is not what Headley means. His claim is not merely that the West is different from every other civilization in the sense in which Tom, Dick, and Harry are different from each other but that the difference is somehow unique. And that is what I do not understand: what makes a difference unique? What makes a difference different from all other differences? Until I know the answer to that question, I shall go on not knowing what I am supposed to think when I am told about Western exceptionalism.

I find it just as hard to tell what Headley means by Western universalism. How can it be universal if it is Western, and how can it be Western if it is universal? I suppose he means that people in the West have or had some special grasp of universal principles. But if the grasp is special, what makes the principles universal? The say-so of the West is no good evidence for their universality unless there is some kind of proof. For every Western say-so can be matched with the say-so of every tribe of human beings that ever thought its members were the only human beings worth the title. Assume there is such proof. Assume that Western claims to universality can be shown to rest on something better than the narrow and self-centered points of view from which most agglomerations of human beings, no matter how small or how large, tend to judge whoever does not count among their numbers. Assume it can be demonstrated to the satisfaction of the entire world that people in the West have actually developed a special grasp of universal principles. If everyone agrees, what makes the universalism Western? Is *Western universalism* not an oxymoron?

These questions may seem sophomoric. But they are serious. I raise them not because I have some canny answer up my sleeve, not because I would like to change the subject from history to philosophy, and not because I want to confuse the issue with trifles and frivolities. I raise them because terms like *Western exceptionalism* and *Western universalism* seem to conceal conceptual problems that are built into the study of history itself. Invoking them in answers to questions about the past without solving those problems makes it only too likely that the most-basic questions about the history of the West will be begged.

The second reason why I cannot quite agree with Headley's case is that it does seem to me to beg some basic questions. A plausible formulation of one such basic question is: "What really happened in the West?" Headley seems, if not to know exactly, at least to have a pretty good idea. His answer, greatly abbreviated to be sure, but not, I hope, abbreviated to the point of totally unfair misrepresentation, is: "What really happened in the West is something exceptional, universal, and deserving of more respect than it has lately gotten, namely the development of a tradition of true religious and cultural neutrality in the name of a common humanity. That tradition is seen most immediately in the early distinction of moral from political authority in the thought of, among others, St. Augustine; it is seen most clearly in the Renaissance and in the development of human rights to which all people nowadays aspire; and it is difficult to grasp without genuine attention to political history." I don't particularly want to disagree with that. It may be brief, but brief does not mean false or meaningless. I have no trouble with short answers to straightforward questions. Though art is long and life is short, few statements about the history of scholarship can be less difficult to prove than that there usually is abundant time to make short answers longer without making them better. I just do not believe that Headley's answer rises to the level of the question.

Perhaps there was a time when that kind of answer was or would at least have seemed sufficient, say, in the nineteenth century, when political history commanded the attention of historians and when the Renaissance was first described and valued in the manner Headley approves. That was a time when Europeans could with a certain degree of plausibility congratulate themselves on having brought a uniquely universal civilization to the rest of the globe. But since then many things have happened to destroy such plausibility. One is the havoc Europe wrought on itself and the rest of the world during the twentieth century. Another is the increasing confidence with which the people whom the West proposed to civilize have turned the tables on the West by asking a straightforward question: by what right has the West claimed a form of superiority over the Rest that conflicts with the West's own proclamations of equality? Yet another is the environment. The human race is busily producing novel ways of changing the face of the Earth, altering the temperature of the atmosphere, and otherwise causing changes to the environment whose character and consequences are feared by some and welcomed by others but in any case impossible to tell with certainty. These changes are in considerable measure due to the impact of Western technology and science. As a result the question of what really happened in the West has become more difficult to answer than once seemed to be the case. It is, in fact, wide open.

In saying so I do not mean to contest the truth of the particular points that Headley makes. I am quite happy to agree that St. Augustine's distinction between the spiritual and the temporal realm, the Renaissance, the political history of Europe, geography, cartography, and other such matters deserve the attention he wishes to pay to them. That part of the argument does not give me much trouble. Neither does the notion that there is such a thing as "the West." I am not sure how it is best defined in chronological and geographical terms, nor do I have much confidence that "the West" is what it should be called. But the notion that the history of the world during the last ten thousand years or so is best understood as the history of a number of what Ernest Gellner called "agroliterate civilizations" of different size and complexity seems as indisputable to me as the idea that "the West" is one of them and that all of them are being rapidly displaced by an unprecedented global form of human society. I do not even mind paying my respects to Western civilization so long as I may treat the others with the same respect.

The trouble starts when Headley seeks to capture what is essential about the West: "The great legacy of our civilization appears to be less in its science and technology and more in the unifying force and challenge, the aspiration to a comprehensive political community, that cuts through the myriad instances of localism and tribalism cluttering the geodetic surface. It is this aspiration that had the capacity to transcend the culturally specific in the creation of a world citizenry, if not a world governance."

I have no strong objections to praising the West for its exceptional drive toward creating a world citizenry but only so long as the world wars and the Holocaust are prominently featured in that drive. Do we really know for certain that the horrors of the twentieth century can be excluded from the consequences of the Renaissance? I do not know by what criterion they could.

Did Western progress in science and technology unwittingly open a Pandora's box of calamities that will spell the end of civilization just as soon as the ice caps melt and humanity is subjugated by genetically modified monsters from the lab of Frankenstein? The time for answering that question has not yet arrived. Do we know that the development of natural law is utterly unrelated to the pride with which it was so often violated by the same Europeans who invented it? John Stuart Mill was convinced that "despotism is a legitimate mode of government in dealing with barbarians, provided the end be their improvement, and the means justified by actually effecting that end."[1] But today it has become so difficult to tell just who is the barbarian and what constitutes improvement that no amount of faith in the justice of human rights and the role of Western civilization in demonstrating their justice can suffice to tell us what really happened in the West, much less establish its religious and cultural neutrality.

When asked about the impact of the French Revolution, Zhou Enlai is supposed to have replied, "It is too soon to tell." The same is true for the question about the legacy of the West: it is too soon to tell—too soon to tell whether or not what really happened was that the West invented human rights; left yet another testament to human folly, one possibly larger and more modern than, but otherwise quite like, the Tower of Babel; created the first global community; paved the way toward the desolation of the planet; or any number of other possibilities. The indefinite nature of those possibilities ought not to trouble historians. To the contrary it should delight them, because it assures that their services will continue to be required for much time to come. But unless I misunderstood the argument, it does pose a problem for Headley's case.

Headley's case is built on the assumption that it is not too soon to tell. He seems certain that had it not been for Western civilization, no one else would have aspired to a comprehensive political community cutting through localism and tribalism. That is laying claim to knowledge of a kind we cannot really have. It also fails to reckon with the extent to which historical events ongoing in the present can change the meaning of the past. It underrates the case of Mr. Jourdain, who did not know that all along he had been speaking prose, no matter how thoroughly he had perhaps recorded everything he said. Mr. Jourdain first needed to be told just what the record was. Unless I am mistaken Headley neglects the possibility that some such need exists. He certainly allows that the historical record is incomplete and will require further scrutiny and that its meaning cannot be completely grasped by individual historians, whom scholarly modesty therefore obliges never to state its meaning without qualification. But in and of itself, so Headley seems convinced, its meaning is a given. That position is untenable. It forces him, quite possibly against his will, to take up the position of an omniscient judge. The criticisms of the West so popular today may well be thoroughly unfair. But by an ancient principle of natural law—the very standard Headley calls upon—no one may be a judge in his own cause, *ne quis in sua causa iudicet,* "because it is wrong to give anyone the right to issue sentence over his own affair."[2] If anyone at all is qualified to judge the West, Western ideas of justice themselves make certain that it is not the West.

The third reason why I cannot agree with Headley's case is that it strikes me as self-defeating. He proposes to recenter the West. In so doing he concedes that the West has in fact been decentered. That concession is the premise for his case. To pose the problem in those terms is to confront historians with a task at which they can only fail. If it is indeed the case that the West has been decentered, historians should state that as a fact. It can then be their duty to explain that fact, to look for reasons why the West has been decentered, to determine the significance of that decentering, and so on. But it can hardly be their duty to lend the object of their study a helping hand in order to restore it to the place to which they believe it is entitled. If they tried, they might succeed in changing the course of history. But changing the course of history is neither their responsibility nor the criterion by which to measure their success. Their responsibility is limited to writing history.

NOTES

1. John Stuart Mill, *On Liberty and Other Writings,* ed. Stefan Collini (Cambridge, U.K.: Cambridge University Press, 1989), 13–14.

2. John Stuart Mill, "Generali lege decernimus neminem sibi esse iudicem vel ius sibi dicere debere. In re enim propria iniquum admodum est alicui licentiam tribuere sententiae," *Codex Justinianeus,* 3.5.1.

Decolonizing "Western Exceptionalism and Universality" One More Time

John M. Hobson

In "Western Exceptionalism and Universality Revisited" John Headley voices his disapproval of the recent "fashionable trend" that seeks to *decenter*— or, if I may take the liberty of deploying such "fashionable jargon," to *decolonize*—the West in world history. He laments as one of the "big losers" of historiography in the last two decades the "dignity" of Western civilization and complains that we now see as "condemned" the exceptionalism and universalism of the West. In the face of this trend that, he insists, defies the actual historical record, he seeks to *recenter the West* in the story of the rise of the global regime of inclusive, universal human rights. In particular he bemoans the seeming disappearance of one of the "seminal moments" in the history of human rights—the European Renaissance. And he counters by relating a Western narrative, in which the creation of a unified mankind armed with the inclusive weapon of universal human rights stems back to ancient Greece and then progresses forward through a predominantly linear series of developments that unfolds within the West to culminate in the 1948 Universal Declaration of Human Rights.

Upon reading his essay I was struck immediately not so much by the rights and wrongs of his account but more by his desire to reverse the "fashionable trend" and restore the West to its "proper" place at the center of progressive global history. Yet Headley does not refer to any of the literature that has raised his ire. His approach takes us back to the *status quo ante* of an unreconstructed Eurocentrism. But the debate has moved on, particularly since 1998 when David Landes's *Wealth and Poverty of Nations* was published.

From *Historically Speaking* 9 (November/December 2007).

While Headley is surely entitled to his argument, I believe he could have made it much more forcefully had he shown us why the recent non-Eurocentric contributions are inadequate. For returning us to the *status quo ante* merely invites a reiteration of the non-Eurocentric arguments against which he has hitherto provided no defense.

Headley's perception of a demonization of the West that requires exorcizing is in one sense curious. For in my view at least the non-Eurocentric literature, though certainly growing, is still very much a minority voice, and none of the relevant books sell on anything like the scale of Landes's text, which is surely the most explicitly Eurocentric book published in the last decade. And it sells in large part because it tells a heartwarming story that many Westerners want to hear. Seen in this light, then, I detect a sense of Western insecurity underlying such a project.

My perception is reinforced by the fact that the end of the Cold War elicited, *inter alia,* two high-profile Eurocentric reactions in the West. The first was a vitriolic sense of Western triumphalism, typified by Francis Fukuyama's *End of History.* The second took the form of an angst-ridden sense of Western defensiveness, found most clearly in Samuel Huntington's *Clash of Civilizations.* Huntington's insistence that the "uniqueness" of Western civilization must be preserved in the face of a rising Sino-Islamic civilizational threat echoes the argument made by Alfred Thayer Mahan in his 1897 essay "A Twentieth-century Outlook," in which he advocated a racial struggle in order to protect Western civilization against a rising Sino-Islamic civilizational threat.[1] Is Headley, like Huntington and Mahan before him, motivated by a sense of Western insecurity that elicits the need to reassert the so-called uniqueness of the West? What *is* clear is that, like his predecessors, Headley reasserts an unreconstructed Eurocentric narrative.

Eurocentrism separates the East from the West, imbuing the latter with all manner of progressive characteristics and the former only with regressive features.[2] The upshot is to pronounce the West as the realm of light, of politico-economic freedom and progressive human rights, while denigrating the East as the zone of darkness, of political despotism, slavery, and regressive human wrongs. This culminates in the final move that casts the West as the sole engine of global progress. If the East is to have a chance of progressing, it has no choice but to await the arrival of the enlightened West, which, fueled by a Messianic white man's burden, bequeaths the gift of civilization— in this case, equality and human rights. It is this exact discursive set of moves that we find lying at the heart of Headley's narrative; one that reasserts the primacy of the West while denigrating the dignity of the East.

Of course the fact that an approach is Eurocentric does not mean that it is moribund from the outset. But the problem with Headley's essay is that it draws from a highly selective and parochial historical record. The story of the rise of human rights cannot be related solely through a narrative that is endogenous to Europe or the West.

For this obscures the manifold ways in which the East has intervened and shaped the West, which has developed in the last two-and-a-half millennia by adapting and assimilating numerous Eastern ideas and inventions. Further Headley's narrative fails to recognize the paradox that the general thrust of the West in its adoption of a progressive humanism has occurred very much in tandem with a Western imperialism that explicitly entailed the denial of human rights and the extension of human wrongs to the non-Western world. Moreover Eastern resistance in the face of the West's refusal to extend human rights to the non-West has played an important part in the story of the universalization of human rights.

Headley begins with the geographical insights that Ptolemy bequeathed, the legacy of which would later be rekindled during the Italian Renaissance. The cartographical and mathematical genius of Ptolemy, he argues, was responsible for Renaissance Europe's breakthroughs in navigation. And, in turn, this made possible the subsequent phase of European expansion that set global humanity on an ineluctable path toward a progressive unification. What this obscures, however, is that the world was not segmented into various isolated civilizations prior to the Iberian voyages; it was significantly interconnected. Elsewhere I have spoken of the Afro-Asian Age of Discovery that unfolded after 500 B.C.E. and was consolidated between 650 and 1000. During that period Indians, Chinese, Indonesians, Middle Eastern Muslims, and Africans were in direct trading contact, exchanging not just commodities but all manner of polycivilizational ideas and inventions. And critically many of these seeped into the West to inform its development, as they diffused across the Islamic "bridge of the world" that linked the East with Europe.[3] One clear example of this can be found in the case of the Renaissance.

A key problem with the term *European Renaissance* is its adjective. For there is now a significant body of research, none of which seems to be recognized by Headley, that reveals the many Eastern ideas—Chinese, Indian, Egyptian, and above all Middle Eastern—that seeped into Europe and helped promote the epistemic revolution that unfolded in Italy.[4] That the Renaissance was indeed a vital turning point in Western history is surely correct; that it was the result of *purely* European genius now appears as surprisingly parochial. Almost all of the ideas and technologies upon which Europe's navigational revolution rested were borrowed from the Islamic Middle East and

India. These included the refinement of geometry and trigonometry, latitude and longitude tables, lunar charts and solar calendars, as well as navigational technologies/techniques such as the astrolabe, the quadrant, and the lateen sail.[5] Still none of this should be particularly surprising given that the Arabs, Persians, and Indians had undertaken oceanic sailing for several millennia before Columbus crossed the Atlantic. This fact helps explain why it was a Muslim Gujarati pilot (Kanha) who guided Vasco Da Gama safely across to Calicut on the latter's maiden voyage. Moreover the optical theory, which proved central to so many of the Renaissance's geographical (and artistic) breakthroughs, was in fact developed by a Muslim, Ibn al-Haytham (Alhazen), who blended Ptolemy's ideas with those developed in India and the Middle East into a higher form of knowledge.[6] It is also notable that the design of the Iberian ships was significantly influenced by Chinese inventions, including the sternpost rudder / square hull and multiple masts.

None of this is to say that the Europeans did not have a creative input or to deny that Muslims and Indians worked with Ancient Greek ideas. But it is to say that the Europeans often adapted others' ideas rather than coming up with them all by themselves.[7] Even Ancient Greek mathematics and science were significantly influenced by earlier ancient Egyptian innovations.[8] Accordingly this raises one of world history's great counterfactuals: in the absence of this Eastern help the Iberians might have remained confined to the backwater of the Mediterranean, with the rest (comprising the "Columbian epoch" and the so-called Vasco Da Gama epoch of Asia) *not* being history, so to speak.

Headley considers the development of law and the idea of human rights. Here he focuses on the European encounter with the Amerindians after 1492 and emphasizes the legal formulations initially laid down by Francisco de Vitoria. Though this was indeed a seminal moment, Headley's portrayal of Spanish tolerance for the "Indians" is one that these latter peoples would have surely failed to recognize. In fact Vitoria was seminal for precisely the opposite reason to that offered by Headley: namely that he set up a "standard of civilization" discourse by pronouncing that Europe was superior because Western civilization was founded on reason. Indians lacked reason, he argued, so they were not deserving of equal treatment and human rights. Vitoria's imperial discourse was also founded on the "social efficiency" idea, which asserted that if nonwhite populations failed to develop their own (natural) resources productively, then the Spanish had a legitimate right, if not duty, to go and develop them with or without the consent of the relevant native populations. And should the natives resist, he concluded, the Western imperialists had every right to wage war upon them. The social efficiency argument was reiterated continuously by prominent European thinkers and international lawyers—including Hugo Grotius and John Locke whom Headley also singles out—right down to 1945.

Headley argues that natural law became increasingly secularized in the hands of the Europeans. This was, he asserts, "of decisive importance, for it made any program of human rights and the vision of a single humanity religiously neutral and hence potentially neutral with respect to culture, preparing the ground for its true universality." But *the* problem that the world faced was precisely the *inability* of Europeans to separate global humanity from the cultural, civilizational context. For the trend that intensified from Vitoria's time right through to 1945—of which the nineteenth- and twentieth-century context of scientific racism was merely a reflection rather than an aberration—was the denial of human rights to those peoples whose cultures did not meet the Western "standard of civilization." Indeed this practice, having been enshrined in European international law, not only justified but also led to the imperial extension of human wrongs—exploitation, war, genocide, among others—to much of Asia and Africa.

Eastern nationalist resistance to empire and Western racism played an important role in the creation of the 1948 Universal Declaration of Human Rights. Eastern resistance was significantly responsible for bringing about the end of empire. No less important the speeches delivered by various governmental and nongovernmental Eastern representatives at the United Nations made possible the introduction of the declaration. Western racism was the issue that spurred non-Western delegates. Theirs was not simply a reaction to an aberrant racist Nazism but was aimed mainly against the Western powers' racist imperial policies, which were the historical norm prior to 1945. Significantly the United States' representatives did their best to water down the declaration, not least for their fear that its antiracist clauses would stir up trouble in the American South. All in all it seems fairer to conclude that it was not "American initiative and leadership" but Eastern initiatives that, in finally defeating American intransigence, resulted in the establishment of the 1948 Universal Declaration of Human Rights.[9]

A universal, inclusive historiography of human rights is revealed only by applying a wide-angled, polycivilizational lens. Headley's "recentering the West" project fails to achieve this precisely because it represents a Western provincialism masquerading as the universal.

NOTES

1. Alfred Thayer Mahan, "A Twentieth-century Outlook," *Harper's Monthly*, September 1897, 527–32. See Akira Iriye, "The Second Clash: Huntington, Mahan, and Civilizations," *Harvard International Review* 19 (1997): 44–70.

2. Edward W. Said, *Orientalism* (London: Penguin, 1978).

3. See J. M. Hobson, *The Eastern Origins of Western Civilisation* (Cambridge, U.K.: Cambridge University Press, 2004).

4. For example, Hobson, *Eastern Origins*, 173–83; S. M. Ghazanfar, *Islamic Civilization* (Lanham, Md.: Scarecrow, 2006); Arun Bala, *The Dialogue of Civilizations in the Birth of Modern Science* (Houndsmills, Basingstoke, U.K.: Palgrave Macmillan, 2006); and C. K. Raju, *Cultural Foundations of Mathematics* (New Delhi: Pearson Education, 2007).

5. Note that while there are vague references to the astrolabe in Ancient Greek texts, it was the Muslims who developed it into the instrument that the Europeans would borrow several centuries later.

6. Bala, *Dialogue of Civilizations*, ch. 8.

7. For a fuller, albeit tentative, first-cut discussion of this point in the overall context of the rise of the West, see my "Explaining the Rise of the West: A Reply to Ricardo Duchesne," *Journal of the Historical Society* 6 (2006): 579–99.

8. Martin Bernal, *Black Athena*, new ed. (London: Vintage, 1991).

9. See Paul Gordon Lauren, *Power and Prejudice* (Boulder, Colo.: Westview, 1996).

PART 4

Thinking about Empire

Empire and Order

Deepak Lal

The Scottish Enlightenment philosopher David Hume maintained that for *any* social life to exist you need order, which has three important aspects: securing life against violence, making sure that promises are kept, and ensuring some sort of stability of possessions through rules of property. Without these there cannot be social, let alone any economic life. Throughout world history order has been gained and maintained in areas that have fallen into disorder mainly through the activities of empires.

Given the confused discourse about our contemporary world order and the politically incorrect aura that surrounds the term a definition of *empire* is needed. I still find Thucydides' definition to be the clearest. He said that in its alliances during the Peloponnesian War Sparta was a hegemon because it only wanted to control the foreign policy of its allies, whereas Athens was an empire because it wanted to control both domestic and foreign policies. Thus empires control both domestic and foreign policies, hegemons only foreign policy.

Not all empires are the same. Machiavelli, for example, observed that the control of the domestic domain of an empire can take a number of forms: "When those states which have been acquired . . . are accustomed to live at liberty under their own laws, there are three ways of holding them. The first is to despoil them [as Jenghiz Khan did]. The second is to go there and live there in person [as in the direct empires based on colonies]. And the third is to allow them to live under their own laws, taking tribute from them, and

From *Historically Speaking* 8 (March/April 2007). This essay is adapted from a plenary address given at the Historical Society's conference"Globalization, Empire, and Imperialism in Historical Perspective" at the University of North Carolina, Chapel Hill, June 3, 2006. A more expansive treatment of the topic appears in Lal's *In Praise of Empires: Globalization and Order* (2004).

creating within the country a government composed of a few that will keep friendly to you [as in the indirect empires of Rome and Britain]."[1]

Direct and indirect empires are more stable than empires based merely on plunder. Even the Mongols had to move to the other two forms of controlling their new domains and in choosing between direct and indirect empire chose the latter. Wherever imperial power has been exercised, indirect empire has always been preferred because it is less costly for the metropole. But most empires have been a mixture. The Roman and British empires were mixtures. Because of the genie of self-determination let loose by Woodrow Wilson, direct empire is ruled out today. I would argue that America is an indirect empire that seeks to control both domestic and foreign policies throughout large parts of the world.

What happened to Europe after the breakdown of the Roman Empire is especially instructive, as it has resonance in what we see today in many parts of Africa and the Middle East. Once the imperial order breaks down, there is great disorder. This is how Samuel Finer, the distinguished Oxford historian of government, has described the economic consequences of the end of the Roman Empire:

> If a peasant . . . in Gaul, or Spain, or northern Italy had been able to foresee the misery and exploitation that was to befall his grandchildren and their grandchildren on and on and on for the next five hundred years, he would have been singularly spiritless—and witless too—if he had not rushed to the aid of the empire. And even then the kingdoms that did finally emerge after the year 1000 were poverty stricken dung heaps compared with Rome. Not till the full Renaissance in the 16th century did the Europeans begin to think of themselves as in any ways comparable to Rome, and not till the Augustan age of the 18th century did they regard their civilization as its equal.[2]

Similarly the periodic collapses of Chinese empires have led to periods of warlordism and widespread disorder until the Mandate of Heaven was passed on to another imperial dynasty that restored order. The Chinese have therefore always placed a very high value on the order provided by their successive empires. In our own times the death of the nineteenth-century liberal economic order built by Pax Britannica on the fields of Flanders led to a near century of economic disintegration and disorder because the British were unable and the Americans were unwilling to maintain an imperial, global pax.

After the collapse of Rome the other Eurasian imperial systems that were not contiguous with Rome continued on their own way. But Europe fell into the bleak Hobbesian state of continual war. This gave rise to a very strange and, in historical terms, very unusual international order in Europe: an anarchical system of states. The lodestar of the subsequent nation-states that arose was the recreation of another Roman Empire, and much of subsequent European history is of a struggle for the mastery of Europe. The relative rise and fall of the various competing European states was linked to the rise and relative decline of the overseas extensions of this struggle: their overseas empires.

This story continued until Waterloo. The British had been in continual warfare with the French in the eighteenth century. The British victory in 1815 finally enabled them to establish their own pax based on the Royal Navy, whose global mastery over the waves created a direct cum indirect British Empire across much of the world. It was also an empire that in a sense was acquired accidentally. For the motives of acquiring empires have been very mixed. Like the Dutch the British Empire was really an accident. In both cases the flag followed trade: commercial overseas-trading companies facing a local vacuum of power in India and Indonesia, for instance, filled it by force of arms, and then Britain had to take on the requisite imperial responsibilities.

But once imperial authority was established, the British created the first truly liberal global order. As the economic historians P. J. Cain and A. G. Hopkins argue in their magisterial *British Imperialism, 1688–2000*,[3] the British Empire was run largely in the interests of the "gentlemanly capitalists" of the City of London. The industrialists, based mainly in the provinces, did not have much influence on British economic and political policies as they could not partake in the glittering metropolitan political and social life that defined the gentlemanly order. Though it pioneered the Industrial Revolution, Britain was soon to be overtaken by the United States as the industrial leader. Britain, however, remained paramount in the business of the gentlemanly capitalists: the provision of international services like shipping, insurance, and above all finance.

These were the economic sinews of British power, and the empire interwove a huge worldwide web of trade and commerce centered in London and protected by the Royal Navy. Wherever possible imperial interests were protected by indirect means. Thus Latin America was never colonized; but when people like the Argentines refused to pay their foreign debts, a British warship would appear and fire a few shots across at Buenos Aires. The customs duties were duly put in charge of British representatives to repay the debt. As Lord Palmerston made clear, the acquisition of the empire and the maintenance of a global order were in British interests because "it is the business of government to open and secure the road for the merchant."

The imperial role was not confined to these purely commercial pursuits. In its newly acquired exotic possessions, particularly India, as the colonial secretary, Frederick John Robinson, Viscount Goderich, declared in 1833, the aim was "to transfer to distant regions, the greatest possible amount both of the spirit of civil liberty and the forms of social order to which Great Britain is chiefly indebted for the rank she holds among the civilized nations."4 This was to be accomplished by exporting its gentlemanly code, in part by creating a landed gentlemanly elite in the colonies and also by exporting the British gentlemen being turned out by the public schools and the ancient universities as Platonic Guardians to govern an empire on which the sun never set. The purpose of the empire was to make the world secure for the gentlemen and capitalism.

The pillars of this global, liberal, international economic order were, first, free trade, which Britain implemented unilaterally. Second, free mobility of capital and labor. The gold standard created a very large economic space with a common currency in which there was also completely free mobility of labor, with large migrations from Asia to work on the plantations in the Caribbean, Latin America, and Asia. Third, and equally important, was the set of treaties creating a global system of international property rights.

What were the effects of this global, liberal, international economic order on the Third World? Despite the nationalist claims to the contrary,5 this was the era when much of the Third World experienced modern, intensive growth with a sustained rise in per capita incomes. The work of the Yale development economist Lloyd Reynolds supports the view that most of the Third World countries first saw a sustained rise in their per capita income (intensive growth) during the nineteenth century, the period of liberal, international order that witnessed the global implementation of free trade, free capital and labor movements, and the establishment of an international legal system. In my view, this nineteenth-century liberal economic order provided the first, most successful, and most comprehensive development plan to date.

Britain's economic hegemony (in terms of relative GDP) only lasted from 1820 to 1870. By 1870 the United States had taken off as an industrial and financial power, and after its unification under Bismarck Germany, too, was a serious challenger of Britain's economic hegemony. But from 1870 onward it is clear that the United States was to be the dominant economic and military power. By 1915–16 it was quite clear that the previously unchallenged British preeminence in finance and commerce, the economic sources of its power, was under serious threat from America. With the replacement of London by New York as the world's financial capital after World War I the British

Empire was doomed.[6] Only America had the means in terms of economic and military power to maintain a pax. But after World War I the Americans were unwilling to take on the imperial role. Instead Wilson sought to maintain the peace through his deeply flawed notion of collective security upheld by the limp League of Nations and enforced by collective sanctions.

It is instructive at this point to think of a counterfactual history of the twentieth century. Suppose in 1905 or thereabouts the Americans had joined the British in maintaining a joint Anglo-American pax. A good case can be made for saying that all the travails, all the terrible things that happened in the last century might not have happened. The joint industrial and military might of an Anglo-American imperium run, let us say, by the equivalent of a Lord Palmerston, could have prevented the kaiser's gamble to achieve mastery in Europe, and one of the most pointless wars—World War I—could perhaps have been averted. This in turn could have prevented the events that led to the rise of Hitler. Similarly a joint Anglo-American imperium might have prevented the rise of the Bolsheviks. The rise of the two illiberal creeds, fascism and communism, that have blighted the lives of millions could perhaps have been prevented. Instead Wilson at Versailles destroyed the Age of Empire and, with the United States retreating into isolationism, left global disorder and economic disintegration to rule for nearly a century during the Age of Nations.

By the end of World War II it was clear that the British did not have the means to maintain the global pax. The Americans had come to realize that all the problems of the interwar years were largely due to their unwillingness to accept their incipient imperial responsibilities after World War I. A bipartisan foreign-policy elite saw the mistake of Wilsonian idealism. By proclaiming the end of empire and ushering in the age of nations Wilson had let the genie of national self-determination out of the bottle. Consequently America —at first surreptitiously and recently more openly—has taken over the task of maintaining an imperial pax. Not merely its relative economic strength but also its ability to transform this into military power leaves it as the only power capable of maintaining the global pax. The Americans today have both a technological and economic preponderance that is uncontestable for at least the rest of the century. Also, unlike much of the rest of Europe, Russia, and Japan and in the near future China, the United States is forecast to have not a declining but a rising population, largely through immigration.

Thus today there is again an imperial power that has an economic and military predominance unseen since the fall of Rome. The United States is indubitably an empire. It is more than a hegemon as it seeks control over not only foreign but also aspects of domestic policy in other countries. But it is an informal and indirect empire. After its nineteenth-century colonial adventure in the Philippines, it has not sought to acquire territory. Nor is it, like the Spanish and many of the ancient predatory empires, a tribute-seeking empire. It is an empire that has taken over from the British the burden of maintaining a pax to allow free trade and commerce to flourish. This pax brings mutual gains. The United States, like the British in the nineteenth century, has borne much of the costs of providing this global public good, not because of altruism but because the mutual gains from a global, liberal, economic order benefit America and foster its economic well being. It has not yet in this promotion of globalization or global capitalism—as some would derogatively label it—been forced to take direct control permanently over areas that have fallen into the black hole of domestic disorder, as was the case, for instance, with the British takeover of the crumbling Moghul Empire in eighteenth-century India.

But the American imperium faces disorder in two broad regions of the world: first, the vast region spanning the Islamic world in the Middle East and Central Asia and second, the continent of Africa. September 11 showed how failed states can provide a safe haven for terrorists who can directly threaten life and property in the American homeland. The maintenance of international order thus means ensuring that there is also domestic order in states that, if they fail, could become terrorist havens.

In fulfilling this imperial mission the United States has recently fought two short and successful wars in Afghanistan and Iraq. But so far it has only imperfectly succeeded in restoring and maintaining domestic order. The aftermath of the successfully completed military campaigns has also revealed the Achilles heel of the American imperium. The United States has created the military structures to project its power, but it has failed to build the complementary imperial administrative structure required to run an empire. Its failure to establish order in post-Saddam Iraq shows up this lacuna starkly. The simultaneous dismantling of the only two national institutions that had (however brutally) maintained order in the past—the Iraqi army and the Baath Party—without having replacements in the wings, shows either a breathtaking naïveté or an erroneous belief based on Wilsonianism that once freed of the tyrant Iraqis would flock to the democratic and humanist banner of their liberators, generating a spontaneous order.

Equally disturbing is the desire of all the participants in U.S. foreign policy to wrap themselves in the Wilsonian mantle. It seems that Americans find it difficult to give up their moral self-image of the shining city on the hill.

They seek to impose their "habits of the heart" on a recalcitrant world in the name of values that are proclaimed as universal but are patently not. As I have argued in *Unintended Consequences,* what are being touted as universal values are nothing else but the culture-specific values of a monotheistic, egalitarian, proselytizing religion. They are not in consonance with what I call the cosmological (as contrasted with material) beliefs[7] of other Eurasian civilizations. These Western habits of the heart—particularly in the domestic domain— arose from a change in the West's cosmological beliefs, a shift from a common Eurasian pattern of "communalism" to the novel idea of individualism. Forcing people with different cosmological beliefs to accept those of the West can only invite fierce resistance and global disorder. Part of the Islamist rage is fueled by what Muslims see as the attempt by the West to use globalization as a Trojan horse to change their cosmological beliefs, particularly in the domestic domain concerning sex and marriage.

Similarly the legitimacy of different political forms is governed by the cosmological as much as the material beliefs of different cultures.[8] Democracy, currently touted as the panacea for the world's ills, does not necessarily promote either peace or prosperity. Moreover political freedom is not the most important component of the ambiguous notion of freedom. We have to distinguish between economic and civil liberties and political liberties. I have argued in *In Praise of Empires* that the former have greater primacy and, arguably, universal validity than the latter, certainly for those who are classical liberals. Globalization, which requires an imperial pax, both depends on and promotes these classical economic and civil liberties. Political liberty, particularly in a majoritarian, participatory democracy, might well not.

So is the American imperium doomed, as many hope and some fear? Economically and militarily there is no sign of likely imperial decay for the foreseeable future. The shortcomings in the administrative infrastructure with regard to the mechanics of empire can be easily remedied. It is worth noting that the British, when they fortuitously acquired an empire after the East India Company's servants had at first plundered the country, decided to educate its servants for the new political tasks they were undertaking. The training system that they created was superior even to that for Britain's own civil servants at that time. In this task an essential part of the curriculum for such an imperial civil service will involve learning about the history and cultures of the diverse peoples who now make up the world.

The major problem for the U.S. imperium is to keep its moralists at home. But with a democratic polity deeply divided by its ongoing culture wars is this likely? As General Vo Nguyen Giap, who engineered the North

Vietnamese victory in the Vietnam war, is reported to have remarked, the North Vietnamese did not win the war on the battlefield (where they were defeated in the Tet offensive) but in the streets of San Francisco and Chicago. It is too early to tell whether the exercise of U.S. imperial power in Iraq will have the same outcome and whether domestic politics will again (as in the interwar years) prevent the United States from maintaining a global pax. But for the near future, despite its faults, the American imperium is here to stay. And it remains our best hope to maintain global order, as the British did in the nineteenth century. It is rightly confronting the major threat to this order posed by Islamo-fascism, and instead of sneering and deriding its efforts in the so-called war on terror the world (and in particular its liberal democracies) should aid and abet these efforts. Moreover as the recent strategic alliance with India shows, the United States is ensuring that an emergent Great Power (China) does not go down the ruinous path that Germany took in the last century.

It is useful to look at the nineteenth-century British and the current American pax from a millennial perspective. Those who lived in Britain during the recent millennium celebrations will remember that their highlight was supposedly the fantastic party given by Tony Blair to celebrate his new Cool Britannia in the specially constructed Millennium Dome. Watching the proceedings on television, as samba dancers from Brazil wobbled their half-clad extremities in front of the queen, I could not help wondering how ludicrous it was that some natives of an ex-Portuguese colony had to be imported to prance about her, when a similar show could have been put on with greater resonance by getting native dancers from her Commonwealth, the toothless association that replaced the British Empire. For if one reflects on the most important events of the last millennium compared with the first, the ascent of the English-speaking peoples to predominance in the world surely ranks the highest.

At the end of the first millennium it was the Arabs who could have rightly had the same sense of achievement, as seated in Baghdad they surveyed the world described by the Syrian geographer al-Muqaddasi:

> The Islam he beheld was spread like a pavilion under the tent of the sky, erected as if for some great ceremonial occasion, arrayed with great cities in the role of princes. . . . The cities were linked not only by the obvious elements in a common culture . . . but also by commerce. The strict political unity which once characterized Islam had been shattered in the 10th century . . . yet a sense of comity survived, and travelers could feel at home throughout the Dar-al Islam—or to use an image

popular with poets—in a garden of Islam, cultivated, walled against the world, yielding for its privileged occupants, shades and tastes of paradise.[9]

At the end of the second millennium Britain was a small island off the coast of Eurasia, whose rise had begun with a few trading outposts established by its merchant-adventurers around the world. Finding a power vacuum in crumbling empires or in empty lands populated by stateless people the British established a vast empire. They led the way to modernity, and at the end of the nineteenth century Britain's dominions and influence stretched to all four corners of the globe. In the last century its outpost in the New World was to further extend this heritage, both economically and militarily. Seen from the perspective of world history, in the last millennium the hopes expressed by Virgil for Rome—

> For these I set no bounds in space or time;
> I have given them empire without end.

—seem to have been fulfilled in large measure for the descendants of this "sceptered isle." Yet in those millennial celebrations in the Dome there was no pride in these amazing British achievements. For in New Labour's modernizing project, Britain's past and particularly its empire has been airbrushed away. But this is a mistake, and it is time to recognize that the British and now the American imperium have offered the best hope of peace and prosperity to vast multitudes around the globe in a congenitally disorderly world.

NOTES

1. Niccolo Machiavelli, *The Prince* (1513; New York: Modern Library, 1950), 18.

2. S. E. Finer, *The History of Government,* 3 vols. (New York: Oxford University Press, 1997), 1:34.

3. P. J. Cain and A. G. Hopkins, *British Imperialism, 1688–2000,* 2nd ed. (London: Longman, 2001).

4. Quotations from Cain and Hopkins, *British Imperialism,* 98, 99.

5. The nationalist claims of the deleterious effects of the British Raj on India are critically evaluated in my *The Hindu Equilibrium: India c. 1500 B.C.–2000 A.D.,* abridged and revised ed. (New York: Oxford University Press, 2005), and Lloyd G. Reynolds, *Economic Growth in the Third World, 1850–1980* (New Haven, Conn.: Yale University Press, 1985).

6. The former concern the world view of a civilization that provides its moral anchor and in Plato's words "how one should live." The latter concern beliefs about the best way to make a living. See Deepak Lal, *Unintended Consequences: The Impact of Factor Endowments, Culture, and Politics on Long-Run Economic Performance* (Cambridge, Mass.: MIT Press, 1998).

7. See Robert Skidelsky, *John Maynard Keynes, Vol. 1: Hopes Betrayed, 1883–1920* (New York: Macmillan, 1983), 325.

8. See Deepak Lal. *In Praise of Empires: Globalization and Order* (New York: Palgrave Macmillan, 2004), ch. 8.

9. Quoted in Felipe Fernández-Armesto, *Millennium: A History of the Last Thousand Years* (New York: Scribner, 1995), 35.

Does Empire Matter?

Jan Nederveen Pieterse

I s empire the main street of history, or is it a side street or a cul-de-sac? In relation to American domestic problems and economic prospects does empire matter? In relation to global problems does empire matter? Does the American pursuit of primacy contribute to global stability, or is it a destabilizing influence? What inspire these questions are the new wars (war on terror, Iraq, Afghanistan) and the recent outpouring of literature on empire.

An imperial state is one that determines the foreign and domestic policies of another political entity, which the United States has done in Afghanistan and Iraq. A second, broad-brush definition of empire is a state that practices expansionist geopolitics. An example of this is what Chalmers Johnson calls the American "empire of bases" and the pressure it applies to Iran, Syria, and North Korea. A third, loose meaning of empire pertains to ideology. America practices ideological imperialism when it casts itself in the role of global judge, declaring American values to be universal values, deciding who is good, who is evil, who is a terrorist and who a freedom fighter, who spends too much or too little on defense, which economic policies are right and which are wrong.

There are two main rationales for empire. A mainstream view holds that the United States as the strongest military power must intervene because it is a dangerous world. This is the overt rationale of hegemony. A reasonable proviso is that American intervention should indeed be stabilizing. The second rationale is control over resources, particularly energy, and strategic real estate. According to Niall Ferguson, "In our ever more populous world, where certain natural resources are destined to become more scarce, the old mainsprings of imperial rivalry remain. Look only at China's recent vigorous pursuit of privileged relationships with major commodity producers in Africa

From *Historically Speaking* 8 (March/April 2007).

and elsewhere."[1] This is the covert agenda of empire, which is here presented in the language of preemptive imperialism, charming for its bluntness yet quaint because of its late nineteenth-century flavor.

A cartoon depicts an electronic signboard in an American town that reads, "Time 10.07, Temperature 76, Reason for Invading Iraq. . . . This confusion is now routine. The task is "finishing the job," but what again was the job?

WMD [weapons of mass destruction], regime change, democracy in the Middle East, the freedom agenda, stay the course, combat terrorism, fight terror there or else it will be fought here, no appeasement—the rationales of war change so often, they are hard to keep up with. In Iraq it is on to plan B also because few remember what plan A was. A technical problem is that the covert agenda is classified and not part of polite conversation.

The disconnect between overt and covert agendas leads to strange contradictions. The overt language speaks of stability, security, democracy, while the covert agenda seeks to use instability, insecurity, autocracy, and Special Forces to advance its ends. Because the actual aims of war are classified, no intelligent public discussion is possible as to whether the aims are being achieved and the methods and cost have been appropriate. Does an imperial approach work in the twenty-first century? I will discuss two dimensions, neoliberal globalization and grand strategy, and then draw up a balance sheet.

Neoliberal Globalization

Does empire matter in light of the dynamics of contemporary globalization? Imperialism is a particularly clunky form of globalization, so nineteenth century. In the twenty-first century does empire make sense at all? Is it a viable project?

Does neoliberal globalization—effected via international financial institutions and the WTO [World Trade Organization]—need empire? If one project is freeing up markets, especially capital markets, does empire matter, or is control over territory and sovereignty rather a risky and costly burden and an unnecessary distraction? On September 21, 2003, the *Wall Street Journal* reported, "Iraq's occupation government unveiled a plan to transform the country into a low-tax economy wide open to foreign investment." If the aim is to transform Iraq into a free enterprise economy, does empire make sense in terms of cost-benefit analysis? In fact if the objective is obtaining Iraq's oil, isn't it much cheaper to buy it?

That there is a "rational" relationship between American military expansion and American capitalism is the assumption of neo-Marxist takes on U.S. hegemony. This is a difficult assumption because economic actors are many and diverse (banks, institutional investors, corporations, government agencies).

The circuits of power overlap with those of capital but not in a linear fashion. Business circles and media have been divided on the Iraq War, with the *Wall Street Journal,* the American Enterprise Institute, and other neoconservative think tanks in favor and many others, such as *Business Week,* the *Economist, Financial Times,* and the Cato Institute, skeptical or opposed. From the viewpoint of corporations the winners are few (military industries, Halliburton, Bechtel, energy companies), many are indifferent unless the cost of military expansion becomes excessive (Wall Street), and many are damaged by American militarism (exporters). The steep loss of American legitimacy represents, in business terms, a failure of brand management. American business groups note with growing concern that American brands worldwide are no longer "cool."

Grand Strategy

It is a reasonable assumption that the wars in Iraq and Afghanistan are part of a wider strategic project. This goes back to the Jimmy Carter doctrine that declared the Persian Gulf to be in the vital U.S. national security interest. It involves long-term American engagement in Iraq (supporting Saddam in the war against Iran), Afghanistan, Pakistan, the Gulf War, abiding strategic interest in the Caspian Basin, and American bases in the Central Asian republics. Pressure on Iran and Syria is part of this. Zbigniew Brzezinski in *The Grand Chess Game* put it in stark language: "He who controls Eurasia controls the world."[2]

However seeking land power on a distant continent is a chancy project. Per definition the supply lines are long. Because of a lack of geographical contiguity and shared history, cultural affinities are slim or nonexistent.

The United States' main ally in this project, Israel, is isolated in the region. Not just the countries under attack but also neighboring states feel threatened, and their regional networks and supply lines come under pressure, creating an incentive to seek alternative security and energy networks. Thus if American designs to prolong the unipolar moment hinge on gaining control of Eurasia, this is a high-risk project, like Napoleon's Russian campaign. Achieving it requires village-level control, but American forces have traditionally failed in overseas ground combat. The U.S. military has been successful in airborne operations and interventions using overwhelming force followed by quick withdrawal but not in sustained ground operations.

The United States tries to compensate for these weaknesses through an ideological offensive of "bringing democracy to the Middle East." American Orientalism places Islam on the outskirts of modernity, devalues Middle East culture, and stars the United States in the role of bringing the region freedom,

democracy, modernity, and security. This strategy ignores the interdepend-
ence of American influence and authoritarianism in the region, ignores the
area experts who counsel that democracy at this stage will bring Islamists
to power, and ignores the clash between ends and means in U.S. policy. Pro-
paganda outfits such as the Rendon Group and the Lincoln Group seek to
bridge the gap and influence Middle East opinion from air-conditioned
offices in Virginia. Public diplomacy Madison Avenue–style with Charlotte
Beers followed by Karen Hughes as top public diplomat advertises a lack of
cultural affinity and is counteracted by Al Jazeera and Al Manar broadcasting.

The neoconservative gamble of using military force to gain control over
energy resources is backfiring. Iraq's oil production, infrastructure, and services are below what they were before the war. Afghanistan is chronically
unstable. American access to the Caspian Basin and Central Asia has diminished due to countermoves on the part of Russia and China.

The American record in the Middle East—particularly its support of
authoritarian regimes whose development record, as documented in the Arab
Human Development reports, is abysmal—is yet another problem. Authoritarianism, corruption, arm sales, and fundamentalism come together in a
package that carries the label "McJihad." Double standards for Israel are part
of this record. Add the American voiceover that declares that the wanton
destruction of Lebanon signals "the birth pangs of the new Middle East."

Forces in the Middle East and the Islamic world have begun to hit back.
Hamas and Hezbollah are democratically elected parties. In this deeply polar-
ized region that, in significant measure, is of American making, technological changes enable both new media and channels of influence such as Al
Jazeera and the "democratization" of means of violence. Nonstate actors can
obtain small arms, Stingers, and in some cases missiles and drones. For various reasons the imperial option has become very costly—in blood, treasure,
and legitimacy.

Does Empire Matter?

My central thesis is that in the twenty-first century the imperial state, the
state that *chooses* war, is a weak state, a state that lacks alternative institutional
resources and imagination to pursue its aims.

Hence in drawing up a balance sheet we must come to terms not with
American power but American weakness. We need to disentangle two dynamics, the ramifications of twenty-five years of neoliberalism and the new
wars. It's not obvious whether we are witnessing the harvest of neoliberal policies since Reagan's rollback of government or just a war-prone administration
that happens to be inept.

Neoliberalism eviscerates state capabilities, shrinks the social state, and strengthens the security state. The mature neoliberal state, after decades of government rollback, is typically institutionally inept *and* a military and law-and-order state. Well before government is "small enough to be drowned in a bath tub"—Grover Norquist's right-wing utopia—special interests have walked away with it. The state is captured by K Street lobbyists and neoconservative zealots who fudge intelligence and war plans by setting up their own shadow-state operations. Hence the neoliberal state doesn't spend less, it spends more but on corporate and security agendas. The weakening of countervailing forces within the state reinforces institutional dependence on the security apparatus and yields a Situation Room world view that specializes in threat assessment and, just in case, threat inflation.

The unsurprising outcome is state agencies that don't function, whether in disaster management, Medicare reform, or drug-prescription policies. The neoliberal state is both war prone (the security sector grows as other state functions shrink) and inept (because of the erosion of state capabilities and the capture of state functions by special interests). Hence the gradual erosion of international institutions that the United States, in an earlier incarnation, helped to build. The outcome is a state that is both inclined to empire and incapable of empire. I have earlier tried to capture this under the heading of neoliberal empire.[3] It marks this era that the debacle of [Hurricane] Katrina and the debacle of Baghdad have become merged in people's minds. Both display government ineptitude, neglect of infrastructure and public services, corporate profiteering, no-bid contracts, private security agencies, staggering mismanagement, and systemic lack of accountability.

Consider an article headlined "U.S. Cuts in Africa Aid Hurt War on Terror and Increase China's Influence, Officials Say."[4] It reports that since 2003 U.S. military aid to most African states and several Latin American states has been stopped because the leaders of these states have declined to sign agreements exempting American troops from the jurisdiction of the International Criminal Court in The Hague. This leaves openings for China to expand its economic and political influence in these regions. This is an example of a state riddled by policy incoherence. The United States places itself outside international law, outside the institutions that it has helped build—the Geneva Convention, the International Court, the United Nations charter, the Declaration of Human Rights. Acting as a global judge *and* placing oneself outside international law are not a sustainable combination.

Thus preoccupied by a conundrum of its own making (including stubborn, one-sided policies in the Middle East) the United States on its fool's errand leaves the global field wide open for other countries to emerge and expand.

While the United States and United Kingdom, the leaders of the war party, are stuck on the path they have chosen, entangled in the backlash it entails (the technical term is dialectics), and duly obsessed by Islamic militancy, the rest of the world travels a different path.

The domestic consequences of the American rendezvous with power include the opportunity costs of empire, that is, what the U.S. government could have done instead of pursuing unipolarity. Economic consequences include the overall neglect of economic policy and the structural loss of U.S. manufacturing capacity. Together with the neglect of education this results in loss of competitiveness and loss of jobs. That the largest American company is a retail company that sells Chinese and other Asian goods with a logistics system that runs on Indian software is a telling sign. It leads to import dependence, an irreversibly growing trade deficit, massive current account deficits, and pressure on the dollar.

Now that the armed forces serve as both an avenue of social mobility (the nation's main affirmative action and workfare program) and the centerpiece of public culture, America is becoming increasingly out of sync with world trends—politically, economically, and culturally. Further as militarism's influence in American culture grows, so does the influence of military authoritarianism. Contemporary American society involves a triple authoritarianism —in corporations as top-down hierarchical institutions (particularly in times of downsizing), in politics because of post–9/11 securitization and the general inclination toward presidentialism and mammoth bureaucracies, and as part of militarism. No wonder that a major American cultural preoccupation is with "leadership."

Empire stimulates regrouping on the part of social forces and countries that increasingly work around the United States. Empire accelerates global realignments. The American preoccupation with geostrategic primacy leaves the economic terrain to industrial newcomers and thus makes space for industrial development in the semiperiphery, as was the case during the interwar years in the first half of the twentieth century when the great powers were distracted by rivalry and war. For some time growth rates in the global south have been much higher than in the north. With this come new patterns of south-south relations around trade, energy, and security.

Military primacy on weak economic foundations means a giant with feet of clay. As the world's major deficit country the United States has much less economic leverage than it had in the past. The wars drag on but American hegemony is already crumbling. The failure of the Doha round, the impasse of the WTO, the demise of the FTAA [Free Trade Area of the Americas], the vanishing act of APEC [Asia-Pacific Economic Cooperation], and the retreat of the World Bank and IMF [International Monetary Fund] signal growing American weakness. Alternative clusters are taking shape that the United States is not part of. For imports and the funds to buy them the United States depends on Asian vendor financing, which will continue until the tipping point is reached, when American demand slips (rising interest rates prompting a slowdown) or when alternative markets, regional Asian markets, and rising domestic demand take shape. Empire matters in hastening American decline.

NOTES

1. Niall Ferguson, "Empires with Expiration Dates," *Foreign Policy* (September/October 2006): 46–52.

2. Zbigniew K. Brzezinksi, *The Grand Chess Game: American Primacy and Its Geostrategic Imperatives* (New York: Basic Books, 1997), xiv.

3. Jan Nederveen Pieterse, *Globalization or Empire?* (New York: Routledge, 2004), ch. 4.

4. Mark Mazzetti, *New York Times,* July 23, 2006.

Analogue of Empire

Reflections on U.S. Ascendancy

Charles S. Maier

I s America an empire? This essay responds indirectly to those readers of my recent book *Among Empires: American Ascendancy and Its Predecessors,* who have taken me to task for evading a definitive answer. In part I did so as an authorial strategy. The question arouses such feeling that a firm answer either way would alienate many readers from the outset. Certainly most Americans today do not think they aspire to empire, although the founding generation of the republic often used the term just to describe the vast dimensions of the country they had created. At a minimum empires imply extensive territory, whether accumulated in one large landmass or in overseas possessions. As early as 1778 the South Carolina patriot David Ramsay had predicted that American "substratum for empire" would propel the country beyond the conquests of the Macedonians, Romans, and British. But the original concept of empire as size was quickly overshadowed. Empire became identified with conquest—a program inimical to the republic for some, its destiny for others. For some commentators the idea of the United States as an empire of conquest seems an absurd proposition. For others, such as my colleague Niall Ferguson, the fact of American empire seems self-evident and not particularly disturbing.

But there are further reasons for ambivalence. I am also reluctant to declare that our country is or is not an empire because I believe taxonomy in the social sciences is always difficult—and often unfruitful. When sociologists or historians identify a social or political category by induction, arguing about whether the category does or does not include a particular case will often be inconclusive. We have had long debates on whether certain countries or individuals are "fascist," whether some regimes are "totalitarian," whether one or another political upheaval is "revolutionary." Such discussions can strain our patience and after a while become tedious. But they can also advance analysis.

Historians like to think that it is only sociologists or political scientists who earn their living by arguing about whether abstractions adequately fit particular cases. We are supposedly philosophical nominalists: if the abstraction never really exists, and no case will fully instantiate it, why constantly argue about it? But, in fact, we historians—like policy advisors or journalists —have to play the same game. Cases are described by reference to other cases. Like the sociologists we argue that a persuasive mass of similarity is present or is not present—similarity in terms of comparable structure, function, or behavior. Underlying all these approaches is the question: What is it like ("it" in this case being the United States' historical role in world politics)?[1] Not every form of knowledge is analogical, but increasingly, I think, a great deal of historical argument tends to be. "Is the United States an empire?" amounts to the question of whether it is like other megastates we term empires. Modern cognition is mired in analogy and analog—not quite the same but both based on recording patterns of likeness.

The problem, of course, is that there is no one pattern or analog. Historical interpretation remains a struggle over the appropriate basis for analogy. If empire means possessing populated colonies abroad, such as the British, French, and Dutch did, then the term makes little sense for the United States. If empire refers not to colonization but rather to a less-formalized search for decisive control by intervening to remove governments we dislike and installing those we prefer, that is, engaging in so-called regime change, then the United States should be reckoned as imperial, although most American policy discourse never describes regime change as imperial.

If the analog of empire refers to political structures at home, that is to a state where the executive is given powers of arbitrary arrest and imprisonment and the representative assembly is reduced to a rubber-stamp role, then there is room for debate about whether the Unite States fits. Most commentators, however, probably separate temporary, wartime emergencies, where "exceptional" control may be delegated to the executive (as it has been at least since the Roman Republic), from regimes that perpetuate exceptional control in times of peace as well as war. To pass through an episode of executive centralization and suspension of earlier civil rights does not entail becoming a different regime. Most such delegations in American history seem to have been temporary expedients, if not aberrations. They have quickly ended. That is why my current answer to the question of whether we are an empire is: "Not yet." Of course the provisional can be indefinitely prolonged—and when the executive claims we shall be at war for an indefinitely prolonged period, the situation is rendered more fraught.

If the analog of empire is a historical process by which rule over an extensive territory is acquired by military expansion, then historians differ over how much a process of conquest was involved in filling the continental landmass the United States acquired from the late eighteenth century on. Must a state geographically constructed, at least in part, by a process of imperial expansion thereby remain an empire? Do the Cherokee removals and the Mexican War constitute, so to speak, a sort of historical original sin?

My own preference is to seek the analog of empire in functional and performative criteria, that is in terms of what empires have sought to accomplish and how they have behaved. Empire, I insist in the book, must be seen as a program launched by elites of different national groups to stabilize their societies by creating spatial as well as social hierarchies. Empires thus are about inequality across a spatial domain; call this horizontal domination. Empires are large enough to have differentiated territories that include a center and a perimeter, metropole and periphery. But empire is also about vertical domination. Empires help keep certain groups wealthy and powerful, and they recruit others by birth or talent to become wealthy and powerful. And empires help assure this inequality within each territorial component. An empire is thus an arrangement, whether negotiated voluntarily or by force, in which elites in the so-called periphery accept the ultimate control of elites in the metropole in return for securing their own local domination. Empires thus rest on collaborators. Empires, though, are not alliances of equals but rather structures of inequality—both domestically and abroad.

Beyond these basic characteristics of structure and function there are the performative qualities that constitute what I've called the imperial syndrome. Let me enumerate several.

Empires tend to pursue a typical spatial dynamic. They enlarge territory or influence to confirm their own new political order. And then they must defend the contested boundaries they have extended to avoid endangering the expansion just attained. Territories once occupied are hard to relinquish. Few managers of empire have a vision of cumulative power. But, like a ratchet, their acquisitions conduce to expanded commitments. Every time an expanded frontier is stabilized, threats come from just across the new frontier. Retreat or retrenchment often seems catastrophic; there is always an unpacified site of disorder just beyond the border.

The imperial syndrome involves a particular relationship to the uses of force. The idea of war evolves from that of a particular conflict to a generalized state of national challenge. Empires are often at war; they often arise out of war; they maintain their domains through force or the threat of force; they often collapse in conflict (in this respect the end of the Soviet Union was a striking exception, although Chechnya reveals that not every region could be relinquished easily); and they leave wars behind them as a legacy—think of Ireland, Palestine, Kashmir, and Nigeria in the case of Britain or the Congo in the case of Belgium. Of course nation-states are frequently at war, too, but it is more difficult for the empire, with its preoccupation with frontiers and control, to forsake the military dimension of statehood. Perhaps empires bring peace to the interior of their large domains. This was Virgil's famous description of Augustus's task: to humble the arrogant, raise the oppressed, and impose the habits of peace. But there is always violence on some frontier, someplace. The state of war becomes the normal state. And there are many advantages to such a conviction: for one thing, it justifies an executive politics. Empires maintain decisive reservoirs of force, and control of that force is what defines the imperial executive. The advent of the nuclear age placed that power in the hands of our executive and, according to some analysts, thus decisively transformed the constitutional weight of the executive.

As a consequence of the tendency toward expansion imperial regimes are preoccupied by frontiers, and politics in the empire is often made at the frontier and then flows toward the center. Military leaders march from the frontiers to seize power at the center; losses at the frontier or even beyond it polarize politics within the polity. Moreover frontiers are never simply frontiers—they are also portals across which the poorer populations of the territories controlled will stream to make a new life within the empire. The imperial syndrome entails a continuing dialogue, often a violent one, between the interests at the frontier and those at the center. Empires thus tend to be constructed in a dialectical process with those who resist. Resistance begins where the borders end and where the claims of rule meet the demands for autonomy. Resistance is endemic. An empire usually confronts at least one site of resistance, external or internal.

So far I've cited only the dimensions of force and power. But empires expand in pursuit of some big idea: the rule of law or "citizenship" in the cases of Rome and Britain; the Catholic Church in the case of Spain; the spread of culture and economic growth or, paradoxically, even the spread of liberty and democracy. Whether the idea motivates or merely justifies gets into nonhistorical issues such as the nature of sincerity. But every successful empire needs a big idea.

Empires have another potentially beneficial value: they can nurture group tolerance, granting religious pluralism or a special role for diasporas: they also allow for enclaves of autonomy within their extensive spatial domains. They often welcome immigrants, especially those from the peripheries that they dominate. North Africans, Pakistanis, and Latinos have flowed into the countries that have often dominated them. Nation-states often impose greater conformity on their peoples than do empires.

The imperial syndrome also involves a particular relationship of rulers to ruled. An imperial regime searches not for discussion and deliberation but for approval and acclamation. It measures popularity. The media replace parliamentary debate, and if there is any symptom of empire, it is the attrition of representative bodies. Perhaps they are formally kept in being—even Adolf Hitler preserved a mock Reichstag. But government by debate loses its integrity and capacity. Granted these tendencies afflict modern democracies in general, especially when they face complex social choices. Indeed the attrition of legislative procedures in a democracy usually arises from the complexity of issues; in a proto-imperial situation it results as a response to alleged security dangers. Parliamentary delegates accept the executive's diagnosis of danger rather than risk being seen as antipatriotic. They pass blanket delegations of power. And even if they insist on legislation, the executive claims the right to interpret the laws that they might pass. Popularity becomes the ultimate measure. If rulers fail in their enterprises, they can lose popularity very quickly. But until public opinion turns adverse, acclamation, photo-ops, spectacular games, and staged pageants replace debate. There are exceptions: rule by committee or by party can continue, as it did in the French Third Republic. But even here the issues that define empire and foreign policy are withdrawn from the arena of debate and discussion. Empire, like authoritarian government more generally, involves the rule of the exception: there is always an exceptional danger that defines imperial politics. The imperial syndrome embodies Carl Schmitt's notion that he who controls the exception in effect controls even democratic politics.

The imperial syndrome involves a rampant growth of privilege and inequality that corrupts civic spirit. Empires can be democratic at home—the British expanded the suffrage as they expanded their empire, the French Third Republic was Europe's most democratic regime, and it conquered Vietnam and Morocco—but empires cannot let their subject peoples share the same democratic ground rules. And even as they may extend formal equality and even income equality toward the bottom, they give the top immense new opportunities for enrichment. This presents grave difficulties of judgment. If millions of middle-income families are each given a small tax rebate, while at the same time several thousand wealthy citizens can each reduce their bill by tens of thousands or more, the redistribution may increase formal measures of equality. But who can doubt which distribution has a greater impact on civic participation? And this is the transaction that the imperial syndrome usually involves: not robbing the poor to pay the rich, although the periphery may be despoiled to pay the center but fobbing off the humble so that privilege becomes more and more spectacular. For a while public games, reality TV, philanthropy, and the admirable but hardly taxing charitable deeds of those enriched may counteract the emergence of populist-class politics. How long that will last is not at all clear.

Let me return to the initial question: Is America an empire? Does it diminish historical understanding, when asked whether the United States is an empire, to say that it has come to behave (at least in recent years and perhaps decades) like an empire and exhibits the syndrome of empire? As a political and moral challenge, perhaps even more than an epistemological one, we must take the current analog of empire very seriously.

NOTE

1. I am not trained as a philosopher, and the philosophical problems of analogy are difficult. But for some recent discussions I found helpful, see Esa Itkonen, *Analogy as Structure and Process: Approaches in Linguistics, Cognitive Psychology, and Philosophy of Science* (Amsterdam: John Benjamins, 2005), 25–35, and Ian Hacking, *Representing and Intervening: Introductory Topics in the Philosophy of Natural Science* (Cambridge, U.K.: Cambridge University Press, 1983), with its skepticism about the uses of explanation (p. 53). Analogies are often constructed with a type of pictorial quality we associate with metaphor (on which there is another large literature) that can pack a rhetorical punch. By using the term *analogy* I am not referring to the similarity of historical situations (for example, whether Vietnam or Iraq should have been interpreted in terms of Munich), but to the underlying tendency to infer and describe in terms of a pattern.

What They Think of Us

A Response to Lal, Pieterse, and Maier

Stephen Howe

O ne could hardly imagine three more sharply contrasting treatments of the same historical theme than those essayed in the preceding three chapters by Deepak Lal, Charles S. Maier, and Jan Nederveen Pieterse. All are in a strong (and positive) sense polemical: a forthright defense of the idea of empire (Lal); an equally sharp critique of contemporary imperialism, coupled with an insistence on its preordained failure (Pieterse); and an argument that though it begins in a more neutral-sounding and coolly analytical vein then moves into a fiercely hostile view of the likely effects of an "imperial syndrome" (Maier).

In the face of such very pointed and starkly divergent arguments it may seem almost quixotic to both offer warm praise for elements of all three and to suggest that, conversely, they all share the same major analytical shortcoming. That, nonetheless, is what I wish to do in this brief response.

The shared deficiency of the three essays is in a word—albeit a somewhat ungainly one—metrocentrism. It might be said that the main reason why the "old" imperial history fell into stagnation and even in some quarters disrepute from the 1950s on is that it became associated in so many minds almost exclusively with the view from the metropole, that of the rulers. In relation to the European empires and especially the British multiple "new imperial histories" in the past couple of decades have sought to remedy that perception. At best they have combined the strengths of traditional imperial history's attention to the global, the transnational, and the interconnecting with

From *Historically Speaking* 8 (March/April 2007).

the insights and breadth both of subject matter and methodological innovation that marked the advent of critical postcolonial scholarship in Asia and Africa. It sometimes appears just at present as though the small flood of research and debate on ideas of American empire is tending to repeat or reproduce the limitations of the old European imperial history. Such a complaint can certainly, in my view, be leveled at Lal's contribution and in a somewhat different way at Maier's and Pieterse's, too.

Lal's essay is in essence, as he acknowledges, a condensation of the arguments in his 2004 book *In Praise of Empires*. Thus it shares both the strengths, especially in economic analysis, and the weaknesses of that fascinating work. Indeed the shortcomings are almost inevitably accentuated by abbreviation, perhaps especially in Lal's central argument about social order. Lal is of course right to remind us that empires have often brought order and security. His mode of argument and deployment of evidence for this claim, however, are not very satisfactory. Citing Samuel Finer—a distinguished scholar of modern comparative government but no expert on ancient or medieval history—as his authority, he rehearses the old and largely discredited pseudohistorical picture that many people of a certain age learned in school but which specialist historians have challenged and largely overturned for decades: that the collapse of Rome led to a centuries-long Dark Age across Europe. Even as the horizon presumably brightened, there was a "bleak Hobbesian state of continual war," apparently lasting until the defeat of Napoleon. (As an aside one might wonder why the little Corsican features so little in contemporary discussions of empire in modern history and is so little applauded by those who write in praise of empires.) All this comes close to caricature; while the other main strand of Lal's argument, that on empire—especially the British Empire—as harbinger of global economic liberalism, is little better in that regard.

Lal's is a radically simplified and startlingly one-sided presentation of Britain's imperial record. He urges that multiple benefits flowed on a global scale from the "liberal empire," including free trade, the rule of law, a uniform code of property rights, honest and efficient administration, and above all unprecedented economic growth. In all this Lal echoes many of the arguments made more extensively but also stridently by Niall Ferguson and, most recently, by Andrew Roberts. The picture is of an English-speaking imperial system that is unproblematically liberal, modernizing, and uncorrupt. It overlooks all the deliberately fostered archaism, the institutionalized, sometimes savage coercion, the "invention of tradition," the pivotal role of racial ideologies and schemata, and the scandal and corruption that so many other historians have found central to British colonial rule in hundreds of detailed studies of different times and places.

The rose-tinted glow of Lal's prose persists with, for instance, a bizarre allusion to "large migrations from Asia to work on the plantations" as an instance of "completely free mobility of labor." These particular migrations actually took place largely under indenture systems that are sometimes hard to distinguish, either analytically or morally, from outright slavery. The notion of Britain's empire as embodying a "truly liberal global order" requires overlooking all that. Indeed it seems a little odd to cite Peter Cain and Tony Hopkins in support, as Lal does, when their work is so full of indications as to how complex, contradictory, and often downright illiberal the imperial project was. As a virtually monoglot English-speaking person I would really quite like to be able to applaud the unique virtues and achievements of my colinguists. But I cannot in honesty do so. In some important respects the "Anglosphere" performs very badly by comparison with other places that have similar levels of economic development. Just as I write, a UNICEF report shows that the United States and the United Kingdom come bottom out of twenty-one economically advanced countries in their records on child welfare. Meanwhile on the two hundredth anniversary of Britain's abolition of the Atlantic slave trade, a report from the Joseph Rowntree Foundation highlights the truly appalling prevalence of multiple forms of enslavement in Britain today.[1] Contemporary Britain has far more fundamental problems than those highlighted in Lal's oddly trivializing moans about the Millennium Dome; and many of those problems are shared with America.

But Lal's case embodies a more fundamental flaw than that of ideological *parti pris.* This is that his views—whether of ancient Rome, of Victorian British imperium, or of U.S. hegemony today—reflect an exclusively top-down and center-out view of history. The ideas about the Roman Empire that he relays come almost entirely from Romans themselves, those who identified with them, or who were nostalgic for the stability and the cultural forms that they believed the empire had embodied. Lal reflects those self-justifying beliefs, apparently without question, and does something very similar in his depiction of British imperialism. It is striking that the extensive apparatus of references in his *In Praise of Empires,* like those in Ferguson's recent books, include barely a single historian or other scholar from any formerly colonized country.

Something of the same top-down and center-out bias is suggested by Lal's references to the "genie of self-determination let loose by Woodrow Wilson" and Wilson's seemingly single-handed destruction of "the Age of Empire."

The Wilsonian moment was indeed a crucial one in opening the way to eventual decolonization, as Erez Manela's important work is today reminding us.[2] But this way of alluding to the ferment of those years surely risks grossly overstating the role of Washington and understating the part played by multiple movements of anticolonial nationalism across the globe. Wilson did not "unleash" these: at most he gave some of them a certain temporary encouragement.

It is perhaps more surprising to encounter a rather similar pattern of attention and emphasis—from such different perspectives—and with such different intentions, in the essays of Pieterse and Maier. Pieterse is no less polemical than Lal, but he is so from an almost entirely opposite ideological position. His emphasis is on American weakness, whether in relative economic terms or as a consequence of neoliberalism's "evisceration" of the state. Empire matters, he concludes, because it hastens American decline. His, too, is a curiously metrocentric view: although he notes some global consequences of the "war on terror," sketches shifting international economic patterns, and even alludes very briefly to the beliefs of those who have either fought or cooperated with U.S. power, all these points are literally peripheral to the argument. His core case is about the fortunes of the American domestic economy.

Maier's contribution is very different in kind: more analytical, less polemical than either Lal's or Pieterse's. And whereas Lal in effect summarizes his recent book, Maier offers an intriguing extension of the case made in his fine *Among Empires*. In particular he at least partially comes down from the epistemological fence upon which that book is so adroitly poised. He suggests still that the United States is "not yet" (fully or unequivocally) an empire. Yet the "analog of empire" and more pointedly "the imperial syndrome" *are,* he now explicitly says, of direct, powerful, and troubling relevance to U.S. affairs, both in terms of its global role and its domestic evolution—though surely few readers of the book had doubted that its argument already tended very much in that direction.

Even Maier's powerful, gloomy discussion of relations between external expansion and internal democracy, however, places its main emphasis on the domestic aspects of the "imperial syndrome": he fears the concentration of power, the erosion of representative institutions, and increases in inequality and privilege. All this recalls very strongly the main thrust of British Victorian radical critiques of empire, which objected to it not on grounds of the rights or desires of the colonized but because it threatened the liberties of the "freeborn Englishman" at home. Equally it surely owes a lot to an earlier generation's arguments in the United States on the rise of an "imperial presidency" in the era of Vietnam: debates that do indeed, perhaps, deserve revival but that seem to provide a rather narrow, even nationalistic or, again, metrocentric basis for an analysis or critique of empire.

Thus far mine might seem a cheap, too-easy, even absurd complaint: Why protest at writings that do not talk about everything all at once within the confines of a brief essay or moan that someone concentrates on the subject that they have announced and intended to focus on? It might even seem, in Lal's rather-tired terminology of mocking political correctness, that I am merely rehearsing a long-familiar gibe against elitist or Eurocentric historical writing. Actually I hope I am pointing toward something rather more complex and interesting than that. Let me sketch, in broadest outline, the argument to which I am alluding.

Maier in particular notes—following a line of analysis perhaps most famously initiated by the late Ronald Robinson—that empires invariably depend on collaborators from among the elites of the colonized society. Yet he does not pursue that thought very far. Robinson's "excentric" theory, followed by many other historians of past empires, views the secret of empire's persistence or decline, its strength or weakness, as lying in the contracts forged between imperial center and local collaborators. Empire could never rest only on physical force—or indeed on economic might or ideological purpose—exercised from the center. The varying forms of collaboration defined the operation of empire at its "point of impact." They were (as Maier, indeed, also reminds us) essentially asymmetrical: if they were not, it would be inappropriate to talk of empire or imperialism at all. But the bargains could not be entirely one-sided or lacking in any significant appeal to or benefits for elites among the colonized; otherwise they would be entirely ineffective.

The application of imperial power thus always involved delicate, ever-shifting balances among coercion, consent, and cooptation and between ideological suasion and interest-driven incentive. Informal empire, or the exercise of what many commentators now call hegemony (in one of the several conflicting meanings of that slippery word) without formal sovereignty, closely resembles formal colonial rule in this, but the balancing acts involved are if anything still more intricate and precarious.

It follows that in thinking about the nature of and prospects for American power today (whether or not we call it empire is, as Maier urges, less important than how strong we believe tendencies toward an "imperial syndrome" to be) we need far more attention to the ideas, ideologies, and interests of those subject to it than is given in most recent, metrocentric North Atlantic writing on the subject. We need far more fully and systematically to think about these *together* with the policies or mentalities in the White House or the Pentagon, in the boardrooms of transnational corporations and the offices of media outlets, or in the changing streams of American public opinion. These are not entirely separate spheres, brought together only in the violent conjunctural clash of particular, often bloody events but nodes in the same network, knots in the same global web.

Central to understanding and evaluating these essays' themes, then, is the need to know far more about the perceptions and projects—including the ideas about America—of other peoples, especially those in places where U.S. power and interest are or might be most immediately engaged. This must be so even if our main objects of attention, as with Lal's, Maier's, and Pieterse's essays, are the centers of global influence and their prospects. What "they" think of us matters even to those at the heart of power.

The interpenetration of inside and outside, domestic and colonial, has been a fundamental theme of much recent work in imperial history. The most obvious form of this is through migration. Sometimes—indeed routinely every day—outsiders become insiders, bits of the periphery enter the center. As Maier suggests, empires "often welcome immigrants, especially those from the peripheries that they dominate." (Though this is certainly not invariably so. Patterns of migration to Britain often bore very little relation to the bounds of its formal empire. The most significant influxes of migrants from former British colonies came when the countries of origin were already sovereign. Very many nation-states have, in both absolute and relative terms, received far more migrants—usually from their neighbors—than have imperial metropoles.) But the inside-outside dynamic also involves the flow of information and ideas. We have by now a vast archive of scholarly work on the empires of the past that explores multiple aspects of all these flows and their legacies: most obviously in relation to the European colonial empires, but we can learn much, too, from study of the afterlives of even the least-known, seemingly most-distant cases.[3]

Far too little in the recent flood of writing about American "empire" has even gestured toward such matters. The three contributors here certainly should not be singled out for censure, because all three display an analytical grasp and comparative awareness far above the average in this recent literature. Elsewhere even when there has not been total neglect of the interaction of center and periphery and the crucial constitutive role of the latter, there has been a woeful tendency toward simplistic or moralizing assertions, often revolving around the crude and unhelpful question "Why do they hate us?" —this is especially pervasive in relation to the Muslim and Arab worlds. One is repeatedly struck and depressed by the sheer paucity of reference in many of the best-known works on American "empire" to any scholarship produced outside the North Atlantic world. Only when, say, Arab scholars directly address questions of American power and do so in a fairly metrocentric way do they receive attention—and then sometimes of a markedly hostile kind. Indeed there are those in American (and, albeit thankfully to a lesser extent, in British) intellectual and cultural life who are unabashedly hostile even to the attempt to hear, to understand, to interpret such multiple voices from "outside."

If we are not willing to include those voices in our conversations about America's world role today, to make them fully part of our thinking about collective mentalities and their relationship to power, then the cost is not only that our debates lack intellectual breadth, historical depth, and conceptual sophistication. It involves us in still graver errors and dangers. The tendency to see all critics of empire as benighted obscurantists or deranged zealots will continue and intensify. We critics in turn will feel ever more puzzled and resentful that our supposed good intentions are so widely misunderstood. In the end we will hear only the echo of our own voices.

NOTES

1. *Child Poverty in Perspective: An Overview of Child Well-being in Rich Countries,* Innocenti Report Card 7, Innocenti Research Centre, Florence, Italy, United Nations Children's Fund, 2007, www.unicef-icdc.org/presscentre/presskit/reportcard7/rc7_eng.pdf; Gary Craig, Aline Gaus, Mick Wilkinson, Klara Skrivankova, and Aidan McQuade, *Contemporary Slavery in the UK: Overview and Key Issues,* Joseph Roundtree Foundation, York, U.K., 2007, http://www.jrf.org.uk/bookshop/eBooks/2016-contemporary-slavery-UK.pdf.

2. Erez Manela, "Imagining Woodrow Wilson in Asia: Dreams of East-West Harmony and the Revolt against Empire in 1919," *American Historical Review* 111, no. 5 (2006): 1327–51.

3. As—to take an example almost at random—from Isidore Okpewho's remarkable work on "memory" in the West African kingdom of Benin, *Once Upon a Kingdom: Myth, Hegemony, and Identity* (Bloomington: Indiana University Press, 1998).

Empire and United States—Power or Values?

A Response to Lal, Pieterse, and Maier

Harold James

"**E**mpire" and "imperialism" are currently used mostly as terms of disapproval. "Yankee imperialism" and phrases like "the running dogs of American imperialism" belong to a vocabulary that originated in Maoist ideology as filtered by 1960s Western radicalism. Given a postmodern turn the language survived in *Empire* (2000), the hugely popular book by Michael Hardt and Toni Negri. It has become the shared discourse of globalization critics. On the other side of the ideological divide few like candidly to term themselves worshippers at the imperial throne, with the result that the rather nostalgic-sounding reflections of Niall Ferguson and Deepak Lal seem to derive from a very backward-oriented mirror.

These interesting articles wrestle with the question of nomenclature and definition, but they are notably focused solely on the issue of empire in relation to the United States, whereas in actuality the problem is a much more general one. Lal and Jan Nederveen Pieterse give strikingly identical definitions before proceeding, in both cases quite logically to diametrically opposed conclusions as to the ethical value of imperialism. Lal starts from Thucydides in distinguishing between Athens and Sparta and observing that the nature of Athenian imperialism was that it sought to control both the domestic and foreign policies of its allies, while Sparta was content to restrict itself to hegemony over foreign policy. Pieterse argues that the United States has a strong Wilsonian tradition, in which security issues are thought to depend on domestic reform and liberalization in other countries. Washington thus comes to believe that the world can only be stable if it shares Western or American

From *Historically Speaking* 8 (March/April 2007).

values. Wilsonianism, whether in the form taken in and after the World War II by Franklin D. Roosevelt or Harry S. Truman or in its more contemporary incarnation in George W. Bush, is thus by definition imperial.

But the problem with this kind of definition is that many states today follow the same kind of logic. It is not simply an American peculiarity or a feature of the mental world of George W. Bush. In fact the underlying logic derives from one of the basic insights of international relations theory about the way in which foreign policies are formulated. Because foreign policy is generally never made in isolation of domestic preoccupations, it is rational for any state that wants to influence its neighbors also to try to shape their domestic policies. Russia wants to influence former Soviet Republics. Most analysts today are in consequence happy to describe Vladimir Putin's Russia as imperialistic. But the European Union and its principal member states also try to influence the behavior of EU members (for instance over whether to admit semifascist parties into government coalitions, as in the debate about whether Jörg Haider or his party should participate in the Austrian government). It does not stop at the boundaries of the EU, however, and uses discussions about membership as a way of forcing its political preferences on would-be members, such as Turkey. Would such (perfectly legitimate) pressure really be adequately described by the term *imperial?* Jan Zielonka recently concluded that "the rise of a neo-medieval empire does not need to herald the end of European integration" and in fact makes it more powerful.[1]

By contrast Charles S. Maier is agonizingly reluctant to make such a determination of imperial character, even in the case of the United States, although he makes the same definitional observation, namely, "If empire refers not to colonization but rather to a less-formalized search for decisive control by intervening to remove governments we dislike and installing those we prefer, that is, engaging in so-called regime change, then the United States should be reckoned as imperial."

He sensibly adds what he calls "functional and performative criteria." Again, however, there is a problem with this kind of approach in that the definition is in reality just as all-encompassing of contemporary political practice as is the wish to shape other peoples' domestic as well as foreign policy. Every state that has ever existed (even radical apocalyptic and millenarian regimes) can be interpreted as a mechanism for the domination and self-perpetuation of an elite. The United States may look particularly imperial to those who think that its elite is not as open as its explicit vision of itself as the land of opportunity might lead one to believe. But there is plenty of discussion in the EU about the nonaccountability of its bureaucratic and technocratic elite.

Russia, increasingly dominated by networks controlled by its security services, or China, still ruled by the Communist Party, or Japan, with democracy but no alternation of the government party, would be "imperial" on this definition. A great deal of the world, not just the United States, now behaves in a very imperial way.

Maier also begins with an older view, "empire as size," which he says "was quickly overshadowed." Yet there is something quite helpful in this definition. In my view it helps to explain why the first decade of the twenty-first century feels so different from the last decade of the twentieth. The late twentieth century saw a rapid liberalization of regulation and a dramatic increase in the flows of goods and capital, as well as migration. This was often described as "globalization" and produced new differences between the small and the large.

In the world of pure globalization small states do best because they are more flexible and can adjust easily to rapidly changing markets.[2] The winners of the 1990s were small states such as New Zealand, Chile, Dubai, Ireland, the Baltic Republics, Slovenia, and Slovakia. But such states are vulnerable, and the historical stage of the past is littered with small and successful globalizers that lost out because of power politics: the Italian city-states of the Renaissance, the Dutch Republic, or, in the twentieth century, Lebanon and Kuwait.

Around the year 2000 this seemed to change, and the new realities were underlined by the attacks of 9/11 and the Iraq war but also by China's search for energy sources in developing countries and Russia's assertiveness in foreign and domestic policy. In today's world it looks as if the new winners are big states with large populations and rapid growth: China, India, Brazil, and Russia. They project power more easily, but they also need to project power to compensate for their weaknesses. In a world in which there is a new preference for power, even moderately sized states—such as those of Europe—are not big enough to act effectively on their own. The helplessness is especially visible in current debates over European energy policy. Britain, France, or Germany (let alone the much smaller Central European countries) cannot tackle issues such as the gas pipeline without a collective negotiating stance. The resulting sense of impotence adds to the political paralysis, especially in countries that emphasize the centrality of democratic control. Globalization depends on a very complex pattern of rules, and rules without compliance mechanisms are useless. But who can be sure that the rules are formulated fairly and enforced equitably? Global systems seem to need global enforcers, but it looks impossible to evolve a satisfactory mechanism for the democratic control of instruments of enforcement. A new sense of vulnerability helps to drive a new obsession with empire. When I did a simple survey of the number of times *globalization* occurred in major newspapers, I found rising numbers of citations until 2000, but after that a fall-off, while the number of references to *empire* and *imperialism* increased.[3]

Modern and rich industrial societies are not used to thinking in imperial terms and bitterly resist imperial implications. They recognize that imperialism has clearly failed in the past and that the legacy of imperialism is a world of resentments and hatreds. Debating empire and imperialism has become much more difficult than the old discussions about globalization. What results is the widespread sense of despair about the state of the world, of which the new debate about empire is a symptom. The despondency is unlikely to disappear until and unless participants in the globalization process lose their current obsession with producing institutional fixes (such as reforming the United Nations or the International Monetary Fund or making the EU or the World Trade Organization more accountable) and think instead more intensely about what common values can hold a global community together.

Here some historical thinking is helpful. Analysis needs to go beyond the polemical use of *empire* as a term of abuse. Ever since Adam Smith and Edward Gibbon published their famous and revolutionary books (coincidentally both in 1776), the history of ancient Rome has been used as a mirror that commentators hold up in order to examine contemporary globalization. An important element in the comparison of past and present empires involves the way in which large-scale attempts to create international order handle the question of the plurality of cultures.

The Roman Empire at first tried to assimilate new areas into its expanding imperial rule by incorporating the local theologies into a pluralistic religious universe. More gods could simply be added to the capacious Roman pantheon, and local deities would sit alongside the imperial gods without rivalry or clashes. Polytheism was based on a deep but politically motivated respect for difference and local tradition. Romans saw polytheism as a basis for imperial rule, so Rome became the center of world religions—not just of the worship of the classic Roman gods but also of the cult of Mithras, Egyptian celebrations, and of course the highly intolerant Christianity. Other great empires made analogous concessions to local faiths: the Qing emperors of China tried to embrace the spiritual power of the Tibetan Dalai and Panchen Lamas; and the Ottoman emperor, even as Khalif of the Muslim faithful, tolerated and authorized Druze, Christian, and Jewish institutions.

The twenty-first-century equivalent, in a world in which the central culture is no longer religious, is multiculturalism: the encouragement of a broad diversity of cultures with a call for mutual tolerance and comprehension. Inhabitants of industrial countries are proud that they no longer just have Western music or traditional cuisine; they patronize oriental incense and mysticisms as well as scent shops with French perfumes. The result has without doubt made modern life, particularly modern urban existence, much more interesting and rewarding.

But it involves the suspension of a particular human facility, that of judgment. Diversity means the enthusiastic acceptance of other practices and a restraint on judgment about difference or the "other." "Judgmental" becomes a damning attribute. The only basis for decision making becomes a contentless utilitarianism, an approach originally developed at the moment when Europe was beginning its universal embrace of the globe. Jeremy Bentham famously argued that from the perspective of the legislator it was important that pushpins were as valuable as poetry.

Rome began to break apart for precisely this reason. Subsequent attempts at universal or world rule (or an approximation of it)—of the Christianized Roman Empire or of the early phase of Islamic expansion—linked world domination with a single set of values or monotheism. But the combination of monotheism or a strong version of a single and coherently defined set of beliefs is likely to provoke continual contestation and clashes.

Integration across large geographic and cultural distances requires well-understood and well-applied rules if it is not to be seen as capricious and arbitrary. If this is true, then the modern drive to polytheism or multiculturalism poses a major problem. Relativism subverts the acceptance and acceptability of a system of rules. This is another way of expressing what I have elsewhere termed the "Roman predicament": and the Roman Empire recast itself under Constantine—in the move that Gibbon so deplored—from polytheism to monotheism.[4]

Modern academic discussions of international order are most frequently based on a functionalist logic. According to this approach international institutions and networks have a legitimacy generated by the simple fact of their existence and that as a consequence can be taken for granted. The order simply generates its own rules in its procedural practices. This approach ignores the ethical foundations that are needed to build legitimacy in a longer run. It leads easily to accusations that policy-makers have taken an imperial turn. There is a limit to the extent that the demand for good politics can be satisfied by essentially internal procedural debates about which countries should be given permanent seats on the United Nations Security Council and be represented in the G-7, G-8, or G-9 or whether voting in the EU should be determined by the Treaty of Nice or by the 2004 constitutional treaty. The architectural debates sidestep the major issues and frequently make for harsher conflicts. Practical experience demonstrates that some common agreement on basic principles is a prerequisite for setting successful agendas in international meetings. Debates that are solely confined to process tend to increase mistrust: Is the agenda being manipulated? Is the other side using unfair negotiating tactics, or are they simply (and unfairly) cleverer?

In the past the most successful instances of benign hegemony involved the elaboration of values that drew other and different societies into a peaceful order. This is the case in the reconstruction of Western Europe by the United States after World War II, an apparently imperial process that relatively few criticize or feel unhappy with. Peace is a value, and it does not emerge simply out of processes. Ancient Rome found the formulation of such a vision completely impossible, and so does any order that thinks of itself as imperial.

As Isaiah Berlin noticed, the eighteenth-century thinkers saw this problem very clearly. Adam Smith was acutely aware of the necessity of formulating what he called "general rules of morality."[5] They were derived from experience, "experience of what, in particular instances, our moral faculties, our natural sense of merit and propriety, approve or disapprove of." Such general rules of conduct "when they have been fixed in our mind by habitual reflection, are of great use in correcting the misrepresentations of self-love concerning what is fit and proper to be done in our present situation." This code provided a natural-law framework for human legislation. It existed as a primary given. "Human society would crumble into nothing if mankind were not generally impressed with a reverence for those important rules of conduct. The reverence is still further enhanced by an opinion which is first impressed by nature, and afterwards confirmed by reasoning and philosophy, that those important rules of morality are the commands and laws of the Deity, who will finally reward the obedient, and punish the transgressors of their duty."[6]

Another way of formulating the Roman dilemma is to ask how to deal with a basic human proclivity for violence. The most obvious answer is that in the process of civilization law (or in other words a system of rules) is needed to restrain violence. Ancient Rome actually found it almost impossible to engage in a systematic elaboration of the fundaments of rule and law. The basic model is given in the Abrahamic faiths by the Ten Commandments. But the Commandments are derived from God, not from an argument about pragmatic necessity or a case derived from the functional logic of increased interaction and communication.

It is important to note that this kind of interpretation leaves little room for the vision made famous by Samuel Huntington. When Huntington's original *Foreign Affairs* magazine article, "Clash of Civilizations," appeared in 1993, it was widely denounced and ridiculed. Since September 2001 it looks to a substantial body of pundits like a highly prescient analysis of the new dilemmas of the twenty-first century. The "clash of civilizations" is another version of the nonglobalization mindset that is currently gaining in popularity. It has a peculiar and mixed pedigree. The notion of an inevitable conflict between an Islamic (or in an earlier, alternative formulation an Asian) vision and a Western one is in fact based on two kinds of argument: first, about the impact of economic and social modernization on non-Western traditional societies and, second, about inevitable and ineradicable cultural differences. In the clash of civilizations a widespread rejection of Western models of modernization follows as a backlash produced by ressentiments generated after the breakdown of traditional order. Ideologues then create and manipulate an idealized vision of the past in order to counter secular progress. But this anti-Western reaction is very frequently cast in terms themselves borrowed from the West. This is the phenomenon that Ian Buruma and Avishai Margalit have in a different context dubbed "occidentalism": the desire to overthrow and overcome Western modernity or "rootless, arrogant, greedy, decadent, frivolous cosmopolitanism."[7]

Depending on which of the above analyses is preferred, different solutions are held out. If cultural differences are really so profound as Huntington suggests, then imperial conflict and conquest are the only adequate answers. If, on the other hand, the problem lies in discontents about modernity, and poverty and marginality are the breeding grounds for violence and terrorism, then a better and more socially egalitarian modernization can hold a more effective cure. Much contemporary debate, especially after September 11, 2001, fluctuates between these poles. Should we fight or buy off the barbarians at the gate? Yet both options look like different aspects of the old but unsatisfactory Roman solution: conquer and provide prosperity. There is only a difference in emphasis. The first is arrogantly belligerent, and the second arrogantly patronizing. Both recommend more power and more modernization.

But there is a fundamental as well as a fundamentalist objection to more modernization (or more globalization) as a simple answer. In the second half of the twentieth century a powerful modernization paradigm became a way of explaining the necessity of progress and development. It was based very explicitly on a means-rational argument, analogous to the functionalist approach to the question of the legitimacy of rules in a domestic or international context. Development was presented by its advocates as a good in itself that would be automatically seen as a good by any intelligent observer. It was not usually seen as linked to any higher value, any way of achieving greater human dignity or freedom. Instead it was a technocratic mill through which humanity was supposed to be minced in the cause of progress and prosperity. And it was exactly the technocratic vision of modernization that produced a new anti-Western sentiment, one that claimed to be more profound and more spiritual than a superficial materialism, while holding out nationally defined styles of capitalism.

There exists an alternative to the challenge-and-response model reflected in the Wilsonian logic. The other path depends on dialogue within a shared intellectual framework, one that is most clearly and uniquely displayed by the natural-law tradition. Instead of thinking that technical development will automatically produce prosperity and thus solve as it were by a kind of magic the problem of values, we need to think and talk explicitly about values. We will identify more commonalities across cultures in this discussion than we initially might have supposed. A symbolic and perhaps important exemplification of unity around values was the lineup at the funeral of Pope John Paul II, the best-attended funeral in the history of the world. Christian, Jewish, and Muslim leaders appeared in a show of unity. The president of Israel shook hands with the president of Iran. The *Financial Times* commented, "There has been little like it since eight crowned heads of Europe assembled for the funeral of Britain's King Edward VII in 1910."[8]

A notion of the commonality of values despite difference might even be extended beyond the brackets linking different religious traditions. The kind of dialogue between apparently rival traditions of thinking—such as the perennial dialectic between reason and faith—offers a way to provide a universal basis for restraining violence that is independent of the chance and necessarily unsatisfactory results of process and procedure. It does not depend on a simple functionalist logic. Our debate must avoid the escapism of technocratic solutions and focus instead on fundamental values.

NOTES

1. Jan Zielonka, *Europe as Empire: The Nature of the Enlarged European Union* (New York: Oxford University Press, 2006), 190.

2. See Alberto Alesina and Enrico Spolaore, *The Size of Nations* (Cambridge, Mass.: MIT Press, 2003).

3. As measured by hits in the databank Lexis-Nexis.

4. Harold James, *The Roman Predicament: How the Rules of International Order Create the Politics of Empire* (Princeton, N.J.: Princeton University Press, 2006).

5. Isaiah Berlin, "European Unity and Its Vicissitudes," in *The Crooked Timber of Humanity: Chapters in the History of Ideas,* ed. Henry Hardy (London: Murray, 1990), 175, 204.

6. Adam Smith, *The Theory of the Moral Sentiments* (Indianapolis, Ind.: Liberty Fund, 1969), 264, 266, 271–72.

7. Ian Buruma and Avishai Margalit, *Occidentalism: The West in the Eyes of Its Enemies* (New York: Penguin, 2004), 11.

8. "Funeral Presents Opportunity to Renew Diplomatic Contacts," *Financial Times,* April 8, 2005.

Empires and Nation-States

A Response to Lal, Pieterse, and Maier

Anthony Pagden

Deepak Lal is surely right in saying that we need a definition—or at least working description—of *empire*. His own, a slight misrepresentation of Thucydides, does not really get us very far. It does not, for instance, adequately describe the situation in British America, where the colonists were, at least until the Stamp Act crisis of 1764–66, held to be responsible for their "internal" spheres of legislation—and of taxation—as were all the Indian "nations" west of the Proclamation Line. Jan Nederveen Pieterse's approach is to assume that the United States is an empire and that everything the United States does is *eo ipso* imperial. This gets us nowhere at all. Charles S. Maier provides a far more complex and detailed tally of what kinds of features the United States would have to have to be considered and empire. These include: the presence of a center and periphery, that is, colonies or provinces and a metropole; social hierarchies; and, crucially, internal allies or, as he calls them, "collaborators," because empires are "not alliances of equals but rather structures of inequality—both domestically and abroad." Empires are also polities that are created and maintained by force and are, therefore, preoccupied by frontiers and the need to maintain them. But they also "expand in pursuit of some big idea." Certainly most empires display some of these properties at some point in their history. But do they all display all of them? The Delian League—or the Athenian *arche*—which Maier in *Among Empires* seems to accept as a true empire (but which, not incidentally, is missing from most subsequent histories of empire, starting with Polybius) was certainly

From *Historically Speaking* 8 (March/April 2007).

concerned with frontiers, had a big idea (the defense of Greek freedom against Persian tyranny), and attempted, at least, to create a metropole (by relocating all the financial resources of the league to Athens). Yet it hardly created social hierarchies or relied upon "collaborators." The Persian Achaemenid Empire, defeated by Alexander the Great, had no big idea, created no hierarchies, and only established a metropole late in the day. Alexander himself may have had a big idea—the unification of East and West—but it was probably provided for him by Plutarch, who was looking at Rome, which does indeed fulfill most of Maier's conditions, although it is hard to see, say, Cleopatra as a "collaborator."

It is also the case, however, that all of Maier's conditions—with the exception of expansion in pursuit of a big idea—can be met by most post-Westphalian European states. Were then pre-Revolutionary France, Spain after the unification of Castile and Aragon, or Britain before the Act of Union empires, in the sole sense that the executive power—but not necessarily sovereignty—was located in one place? Are empires, as Philip Bobbitt has suggested, merely a particular kind of large state?

Two things are missing from Maier's checklist. Empires, like states, have sought to incorporate the conquered or allied populations into one single, if diverse, polity. This was the big idea of the Roman Empire, the Spanish Empire, the French Empire, and ultimately the British Empire. It is not merely a question of seeking "collaborators" or making friends. It is a question of making, as one Spanish jurist phrased it, all the inhabitants of the Habsburg Monarchy from Cadiz to Manila "subjects and citizens" of the same monarch.

The second point is one of sovereignty. Ever since 1648 sovereignty was conceived within Europe as indivisible. Beyond the nation-state, however, it could only be divided among any number of rulers. In most modern empires there did indeed exist a metropole and a periphery. In many cases legislation did indeed originate from the center. But never was the metropole the sole undivided source of executive and legislative authority as it always is in any modern state.

Is the United States an empire? Does it, in Maier's words, resemble the "other megastates we term empires"? I think that the answer is ultimately no. The United States may, in the minds of some of its founders, have had clearly defined imperial ambitions. The westward expansion of the United States was as obviously imperial—and only slightly less ferocious—as the Mongol conquests of Central Asia. And the Civil War was as much a war to compel disaffected provinces to remain within the *arche* as the Athenian wars against Thrasos or Naxos. Beyond its own territorial boundaries, however, the

United States has only ever been an empire briefly: in the 1890s in Hawaii, the Philippines, and Puerto Rico. Except in these places the United States has never attempted to make citizens out of the peoples inhabiting the territories it has occupied or shown the slightest intention of sharing sovereignty with any other ruler. "Regime change," as Maier says, has never been described as imperial, for the simple reason that it is not. And this, as Maier's colleague Niall Ferguson has claimed, is precisely what is wrong with it. There are no halfway houses from which it is possible to conduct intervention without wholesale political reconstruction. And reconstruction requires not only occupation; it also requires the transformation of the state. In the case of Iraq it requires not so much what the British did in Mesopotamia after 1918—which, for all Ferguson's misplaced admiration for it, was not so very different, if rather better informed, from what the Bush administration is currently trying to do—but what the Ottomans had done nearly half a millennium earlier.

There is one further terminological problem with the "Is the United States an empire?" debate. *Empire* is not the same thing as *imperial,* which is not the same thing as *imperialist.* The latter word—along with *imperialism* and *imperialistic*—seems to have disappeared from our vocabulary at about the same time as the collapse of the Berlin Wall. This is a shame. Because detached from their Leninist moorings these terms can provide a useful description of the kinds of things that Pieterse deplores about American foreign policy, without the need to confuse the policy of any given administration with a particular kind of polity. Many states—the Sudan, Kenya, Mexico—can readily be accused of imperialism. But I doubt that anyone would seriously wish to describe any of them as empires.

To answer Pieterse's question: empires—true empires—matter, not least of all because they have been around for far longer than any other kind of social or political organization. By comparison the nation-state is a recent and somewhat shaky innovation that, if the attempts to transplant it to Africa and Asia are anything to go by, may have had its day. Empires, as megastates in which sovereignty is shared and citizenship universal, may, in some modified, improved, and more humane version, be due for a comeback. There are many who think that the European Union, now the second-largest economic power on Earth, is just such a one.

Further Readings

On World History

Bentley, Jerry H. *Shapes of World History in Twentieth-Century Scholarship.* Washington, D.C.: American Historical Association, 1996.

Costello, Paul *World Historians and Their Goals: Twentieth-Century Answers to Modernism.* DeKalb: Northern Illinois University Press, 1993.

Crossley, Pamela Kyle. *What Is Global History?* Cambridge, U.K.: Polity, 2008.

Hodgson, Marshall G. S. *Rethinking World History: Essays on Europe, Islam, and World History.* Cambridge, U.K.: Cambridge University Press, 1993.

Hughes-Warrington, Marnie, ed. *World Histories.* Houndsmills, Basingstoke, U.K.: Palgrave Macmillan, 2005.

Manning, Patrick. *Navigating World History: Historians Create a Global Past.* Houndsmills, Basingstoke, U.K.: Palgrave Macmillan, 2003.

Pomper, Philip, Richard H. Elphick, and Richard T. Vann, eds. *World History: Ideologies, Structures, and Identities.* Malden, Mass.: Blackwell, 1998.

Stuchtey, Benedickt, and Eckhardt Fuchs, eds. *Writing World History, 1800–2000.* Oxford: Oxford University Press, 2003.

World Histories and Thematic Macrohistories

Barraclough, Geoffrey. *Turning Points in World History.* New York: Thames and Hudson, 1979.

Bentley, Jerry H. *Old World Encounters: Cross-Cultural Contacts and Exchanges in Pre-Modern Times.* New York: Oxford University Press, 1993.

Cook, Michael. *A Brief History of the Human Race.* New York: Norton, 2003.

Crosby, Alfred W. *The Columbian Exchange: Biological and Cultural Consequences of 1492.* Westport, Conn.: Greenwood, 1972.

———. *Ecological Imperialism: The Biological Expansion of Europe, 900–1900.* New York: Cambridge University Press, 1986.

Curtin, Philip D. *The World and the West: The European Challenge and the Overseas Response in the Age of Empire.* Cambridge, U.K.: Cambridge University Press, 2000.

Davis, James C. *The Human Story: Our History, from the Stone Age to Today.* New York: HarperCollins, 2004.

Diamond, Jared. *Guns, Germs, and Steel: The Fates of Human Societies.* New York: Norton, 1997.

Fagan, Brian. *The Long Summer: How Climate Changed Civilization.* New York: Basic Books, 2004.

Fernández-Armesto, Felipe. *Civilizations: Culture, Ambition, and the Transformation of Nature.* New York: Free Press, 2001.

———. *Pathfinders: A Global History of Exploration.* New York: Norton, 2006.

Hanson, Victor Davis. *Carnage and Culture: Landmark Battles in the Rise of Western Power.* New York: Doubleday, 2001.

Kennedy, Paul. *The Rise and Fall of the Great Powers: Economic Change and Military Conflict from 1500 to 2000.* New York: Random, 1987.

Lynn, John A. *Battle: A History of Combat and Culture.* Boulder, Colo.: Westview, 2003.

Marks, Robert B. *The Origins of the Modern World: A Global and Economic Narrative.* Lanham, Md.: Rowman & Littlefield, 2002.

McNeill, J. R. *Something New under the Sun: An Environmental History of the Twentieth-century World.* New York: Norton, 2000.

McNeill, J. R., and William H. McNeill. *The Human Web: A Bird's-eye View of World History.* New York: Norton, 2003.

McNeill, William H. *The Global Condition: Conquerors, Catastrophes, and Community.* Princeton, N.J.: Princeton University Press, 1992.

———. *Plagues and People.* Garden City, N.Y.: Doubleday, 1976.

———. *The Pursuit of Power: Technology, Armed Force, and Society since A.D. 1000.* Chicago: University of Chicago Press, 1982.

———. *The Rise of the West: A History of the Human Condition.* Chicago: University of Chicago Press, 1963.

Pagden, Anthony. *Worlds at War: The 2,500-Year Struggle between East and West.* New York: Random, 2008.

Sanneh, Lamin O. *Disciples of All Nations: Pillars of World Christianity.* New York: Oxford University Press, 2007.

Stearns, Peter N. *Western Civilization in World History.* New York: Routledge, 2003.

Walls, Andrew F. *The Missionary Movement in Christian History: Studies in the Transmission of Faith.* Maryknoll, N.Y.: Orbis, 1996.

The History of the West and World in Tension

Blaut, J. M. *The Colonizer's Model of the World: Geographic Diffusionism and Eurocentric History.* New York: Guilford, 1993.

Frank, Andre Gunder. *ReORIENT: Global Economy in the Asian Age.* Berkeley: University of California Press, 1998.

Goody, Jack. *The East in the West.* Cambridge, U.K.: Cambridge University Press, 1996.

———. *The Theft of History.* Cambridge, U.K.: Cambridge University Press, 2006.

Gress, David. *From Plato to NATO: The Idea of the West and Its Opponents.* New York: Free Press, 1998.

Headley, John M. *The Europeanization of the World: On the Origins of Human Rights and Democracy.* Princeton, N.J.: Princeton University Press, 2007.

Hobson, John M. *The Eastern Origins of Western Civilisation*. Cambridge, U.K.: Cambridge University Press, 2004.

Landes, David. *The Wealth and Poverty of Nations: Why Some Are So Rich and Some So Poor*. New York: Norton, 1998.

Pomeranz, Kenneth. *The Great Divergence: China, Europe, and the Making of the Modern World Economy*. Princeton, N.J.: Princeton University Press, 2000.

Wong, R. Bin. *China Transformed: Historical Change and the Limits of European Experience*. Ithaca, N.Y.: Cornell University Press, 1997.

World-Systems

Chase-Dunn, Christopher, and Thomas D. Hall. *Rise and Demise: Comparing World-Systems*. Boulder, Colo.: Westview, 1997.

Sanderson, Stephen K., ed. *Civilizations and World Systems: Studying World Historical Change*. Walnut Creek, Calif.: AltaMira, 1995.

Wallerstein, Immanuel. *World-Systems Analysis: An Introduction*. Raleigh, N.C.: Duke University Press, 2004.

Global History and Globalization

Mazlish, Bruce. *The New Global History*. New York: Routledge, 2006.

Hopkins, A. G., ed. *Globalization in World History*. London: Pimlico, 2002.

Wills, John E., Jr. *1688: A Global History*. New York: Norton, 2001.

Big History

Christian, David. *Maps of Time: An Introduction to Big History*. Berkeley: University of California Press, 2004.

Spier, Fred. *The Structure of Big History: From the Big Bang until Today*. Amsterdam: Amsterdam University Press, 1996.

Empire

Chua, Amy. *Day of Empire: How Hyperpowers Rise to Global Dominance—and Why They Fall*. New York: Doubleday, 2007.

Darwin, John. *After Tamerlane: The Global History of Empire*. London: Lane, 2007.

Hardt, Michael, and Antonio Negri. *Empire*. Cambridge, Mass.: Harvard University Press, 2000.

Howe, Stephen. *Empire: A Very Short Introduction*. New York: Oxford University Press, 2002.

James, Harold. *The Roman Predicament: How the Rules of International Order Create the Politics of Empire*. Princeton, N.J.: Princeton University Press, 2006.

Lal, Deepak. *In Praise of Empires: Globalization and Order*. New York: Palgrave Macmillan, 2004.

Maier, Charles S. *Among Empires: American Ascendancy and Its Predecessors*. Cambridge, Mass.: Harvard University Press, 2006.

Nederveen Pieterse, Jan. *Globalization or Empire?* New York: Routledge, 2004.

Contributors

LAUREN BENTON is professor of history at New York University. Her *Law and Colonial Cultures: Legal Regimes in World History, 1400–1900* (2002) won the World History Association Book Award and the James Willard Hurst Prize.

MICHAEL COOK is Class of 1943 University Professor of Near Eastern Studies at Princeton University. Among his most recent books are *A Brief History of the Human Race* (2003) and *Commanding Right and Forbidding Wrong in Islamic Thought* (2001).

CONSTANTIN FASOLT is Karl J. Weintraub Professor in the department of history and the college at the University of Chicago. His most recent book is *The Limits of History* (2004).

FELIPE FERNÁNDEZ-ARMESTO is the Prince of Asturias Professor of History at Tufts University. He also holds an appointment as professor of global environmental history at Queen Mary, University of London. He is the author of a score of books including *Millennium: A History of the Last Thousand Years* (1995), *Civilizations* (2000), and *Pathfinders: A Global History of Exploration* (2006).

HANNA H. GRAY is president emeritus and Harry Pratt Judson Distinguished Professor Emeritus, University of Chicago.

JOHN M. HEADLEY is emeritus professor of history at the University of North Carolina, Chapel Hill. He has written extensively about the history of early Modern Europe. His most recent book is *The Europeanization of the World: On the Origins of Human Rights and Democracy* (2008).

JOHN M. HOBSON is professor of politics and international relations at the University of Sheffield. He is the author of *The Eastern Origins of Western Civilisation*.

STEPHEN HOWE is professor of history at the University of Bristol and author of, among many other works, *Empire: A Very Short Introduction* (2002).

HAROLD JAMES is professor of history and international affairs at the Wilson School, Princeton University, and Marie Curie Professor of History at the European University Institute, Florence, Italy. He is author of *The Roman Predicament: How the Rules of International Order Create the Politics of Empire* (2006).

DEEPAK LAL is the James S. Coleman Professor of International Development Studies at the University of California at Los Angeles, professor emeritus of political economy at University College London, and a senior fellow at the Cato Institute. He is the author of *In Praise of Empires: Globalization and Order* (2004).

CHARLES S. MAIER is the Leverett Saltonstall Professor of History at Harvard University. His most recent book is *Among Empires: American Ascendancy and Its Predecessors* (2006).

BRUCE MAZLISH is emeritus professor of history at the Massachusetts Institute of Technology. Over a long and distinguished career he has been a pathfinder in two fields of historical inquiry: psychohistory and new global history. He has been a founding editor of two scholarly journals: *History & Theory* and *New Global Studies*. Among his most recent books is *Civilization and its Contents* (2004).

J. R. MCNEILL is professor of history and University Professor at Georgetown University. He is the author of several important books, the most recent of which is *Epidemics and Geopolitics in the American Tropics* (2008).

WILLIAM H. MCNEILL is one of the most influential historians of our time and a seminal scholar in the field of world history. He is the Robert A. Millikan Distinguished Service Professor Emeritus of History at the University of Chicago. A past president of the American Historical Association he is the author of many books including *The Human Web: A Bird's-eye View of World History* (2003), written with his son, historian J. R. McNeill.

ANTHONY PAGDEN is professor of history and political science at the University of California at Los Angeles. He has written several books on empires, including *Peoples and Empires: A Short History of European Migration, Exploration, and Conquest, from Greece to Present* (2001). His most recent book is *Worlds at War: The 2,500-Year Struggle between East and West* (2008).

JAN NEDERVEEN PIETERSE is professor of sociology at the University of Illinois at Urbana-Champaign. His most recent books are *Ethnicities and Global Multiculture: Pants for an Octopus* (2007) and *Is There Hope for Uncle Sam? Beyond the American Bubble* (2008).

ROBBIE ROBERTSON is a development historian at La Trobe University in Australia. He is author of *The Three Waves of Globalization: A History of Developing Global Consciousness* (2003).

DOMINIC SACHSENMAIER is assistant professor of transcultural and Chinese history at Duke University. His research interests are Chinese and Western approaches to global history as well as the impact of World War I on political and intellectual cultures in China and other parts of the world. He is widely published in fields such as seventeenth-century Sino-Western relations, theories of global history, and international political movements during the 1920s.

PETER N. STEARNS is provost and professor of history at George Mason University. He has taught and published widely in both Western civilization and world history. Among his recent books are *From Alienation to Addiction: Modern American Work in Global Historical Perspective* (2008), *American Fear: The Causes and Consequences of*

High Anxiety (2006), and *Global Outrage: The Impact of World Opinion on Contemporary History* (2005). He is editor of the *Journal of Social History* and Routledge's *Themes in World History* series.

DONALD A. YERXA is director of the Historical Society and professor of history at Eastern Nazarene College. He has been editor of *Historically Speaking* since 2001. He is the author of three books, including *Admirals and Empire* (1991), and editor of five other volumes in the Historians in Conversation series.

Index